EXPERIMENTS WITH CHEMISTRY

SCIENCE WHIZ EXPERIMENTS

EXPERIMENTS WITH CHEMISTRY

Robert Gardner

Enslow Publishing
101 W. 23rd Street
Suite 240
New York, NY 10011
USA
enslow.com

Published in 2018 by Enslow Publishing, LLC.
101 W. 23rd Street, Suite 240, New York, NY 10011

Library of Congress Cataloging-in-Publication Data

Names: Gardner, Robert, 1929- author.
Title: Experiments with chemistry / Robert Gardner.
Description: New York : Enslow Publishing, 2018. | Series: Science whiz experiments | Includes bibliographical references and index.
Identifiers: LCCN 2016057567 | ISBN 9780766086760 (library bound : alk. paper)
Subjects: LCSH: Chemistry—Experiments—Juvenile literature. | Oxidation—Experiments—Juvenile literature. | Science projects—Juvenile literature.
Classification: LCC QD43 .G3725 2018 | DDC 540.78—dc23
LC record available at https://lccn.loc.gov/2016057567

Printed in the United States of America

To Our Readers: We have done our best to make sure all website addresses in this book were active and appropriate when we went to press. However, the author and the publisher have no control over and assume no liability for the material available on those websites or on any websites they may link to. Any comments or suggestions can be sent by e-mail to customerservice@enslow.com.

Illustrations by Joseph Hill

Photo Credits: Cover, p. 3, kotoffei/Shutterstock.com; back cover and interior pages background pattern curiosity/Shutterstock.com.

Contents

Introduction

So, what exactly is chemistry? Chemistry is the study of anything that has mass, or matter. Chemists do scientific experiments, following the scientific method, to study the way matter can be changed. You can also study matter by doing the experiments in this book. You will see chemicals combine to form new substances, separate the components of mixtures, watch solids disappear into liquids only to reappear when the liquids are heated, witness the production of electricity from chemicals, and much, much more.

At times, as you carry out the activities in this book, you may need a partner to help you. It would be best if you work with someone who enjoys experimenting as much as you do. That way, you will both enjoy what you are doing. **If any danger is involved in doing an experiment, we will tell you. In some cases, to avoid danger, you will be asked to work with an adult. Please do so.** We do not want you to take any chances that could lead to an injury.

Like any good scientist, you will find it useful to record ideas, notes, data, and anything you can conclude from your investigations in a notebook. By doing so you can keep track of the information you gather and the conclusions you reach. It will allow you to refer back to things you have done and help you in doing other projects in the future.

Entering a Science Fair

Some of the investigations in this book contain ideas you might use at a science fair. However, judges at science fairs do not reward projects or experiments that are simply copied from a book. For example, a diagram of different temperature scales would not impress most judges. Finding a unique way to measure the heat produced per gram of a substance undergoing a chemical change would be more likely to attract their attention.

Science fair judges tend to reward creative thought and imagination. It is difficult to be creative or imaginative unless you are really interested in your project. Try to choose an investigation that appeals to you. Before you jump into a project, consider, too, your own talents and the cost of the materials you will need.

If you decide to use an experiment or idea found in this book for a science fair, you should find ways to modify or extend it. This should not be difficult. As you carry out investigations new ideas will come to mind. You will think of questions leading to experiments that could make excellent science fair projects, particularly because the ideas are your own and are interesting to you.

If you decide to enter a science fair and have never done so, you should read some of the books listed in the Further Reading section. These books deal specifically with science fairs. They will provide plenty of helpful hints and useful information. They will help you to avoid the mistakes that first-time competitors sometimes make. You will learn how to prepare appealing reports that include charts and graphs, how to set up and display your work, how to present your project, and how to relate to judges and visitors.

Be Safe

Safety is essential when you do chemistry experiments. Your eyes require particular protection. Dangerous chemicals or flying fragments can damage them. Therefore, you should **always wear safety glasses** when working with chemicals. Should any chemicals accidentally enter your eye, flood your eye with running water from the spray nozzle at your kitchen sink for at least ten minutes. Then **tell an adult** and call a physician.

A small particle in your eye, if visible in a mirror, can usually be removed by moving it toward the corner of your eye with the moistened tip of a facial tissue. If that doesn't work, pulling the upper lid out and down over the lower eyelashes may wash the particle away. If the particle still remains, seek a physician.

The likelihood of an injury is very small. Most of the projects included in this book are perfectly safe. However, the following safety rules are well worth reading before you start any project.

1. Do not touch or taste chemicals unless instructed to do so.
2. Be careful not to mislabel chemicals. Do not return a chemical to the container from which it came. Discard excess chemicals as advised by a knowledgeable adult.
3. Do any experiments or projects, whether from this book or of your own design, under the adult supervision of a science teacher or other knowledgeable adult.
4. Read all instructions carefully before proceeding with a project. If you have questions, check with your supervisor before going any further.
5. Maintain a serious attitude while conducting experiments. Fooling around can be dangerous to you and to others.
6. Always wear safety goggles when doing chemistry experiments.
7. Do not eat or drink while experimenting.
8. Have a first aid kit nearby while you are experimenting.
9. Do not mix chemicals just to see what happens! Use only the chemicals called for and use or mix them only as directed.
10. Never let water droplets come in contact with a hot lightbulb.
11. Never experiment with household electricity. Use batteries instead.

12. Use only alcohol-based thermometers. Some older thermometers contain mercury, which is a dangerous substance.
13. Immediately wash off any chemicals that accidentally contact your skin with lots of water.
14. Never insert glass tubing into the holes in rubber stoppers without wearing heavy gloves and first moistening the tubing and stopper with glycerin or moist soap. Hold your hands close together to reduce leverage on the glass.
15. When removing glass tubing from a stopper, carefully add a drop or two of glycerin to the hole before gently twisting the tubing while wearing heavy gloves. If the joint is really stuck, **ask an adult** to use a sharp knife to cut open the stopper.
16. Any heated glass should be placed on a piece of wood to cool. Never pick up hot glass. If in doubt, wait!
17. Do not use cracked or broken glass vessels. To avoid injury to trash carriers, place broken glass in a can that can be sealed before discarding.
18. Always wear shoes, not sandals, while experimenting.
19. Wash your hands thoroughly after completing an experiment.

Keeping Notes

Your notebook, as any scientist will tell you, is a valuable possession. It should contain ideas you have as you experiment, your sketches, calculations you make, and hypotheses you propose. It should include a description of every experiment you do and the data you record, such as temperatures, pressures, volumes, weights, and so on. It should also contain the results of your experiments, graphs you create, and any conclusions you reach based on your results.

Following the Scientific Method

Scientists look at the world and try to understand how things work. They make careful observations and conduct research. Different areas of science use different approaches. Depending on the problem, one method is likely to be better than another. Designing a new medicine for heart disease, studying the spread of an invasive plant, such as purple loosestrife, and finding evidence of water on Mars all require different methods.

Despite the differences, all scientists use a similar general approach in doing experiments. This is called the scientific method. In most experiments, some or all of the following steps are used: observing a problem, formulating a question, making a hypothesis (an answer to the question), making a prediction (an if-then statement), designing and conducting an experiment, analyzing results, drawing conclusions, and accepting or rejecting the hypothesis. Scientists then share their findings by writing articles that are published.

You might wonder how to start an experiment. When you observe something, you may become curious and ask a question. Your question, which could arise from an earlier experiment or from reading, may be answered by a well-designed investigation. Once you have a question, you can make a hypothesis. Your hypothesis is a possible answer to the question. Once you have a hypothesis, it is time to design an experiment to test a consequence of your hypothesis.

In most cases, you should do a controlled experiment. This means having two groups that are treated the same except for the one factor being tested. That factor is called a variable. For example, suppose your question is "Do green plants need light?" Your hypothesis might be that they do need light. To test the hypothesis, you would use two groups of green plants. One group is called the control group, the other is called the experimental group. The two groups should be treated the same except for one factor. Both should be planted in the same amount and type of soil, given the same amount of water, kept at the same temperature, and so forth. The control group would be placed in the dark. The experimental group would be put in the light. Light is the variable. It is the only difference between the two groups.

During the experiment, you would collect data. For example, you might measure the plants' growth in centimeters, count the number of living and dead leaves, and note the color and condition of the leaves. By comparing the data collected from the control and experimental groups over a few weeks, you would draw conclusions. Healthier growth and survival rates of plants grown in light would allow you to conclude that green plants need light.

Two other terms are often used in scientific experiments—"dependent" and "independent variables." One dependent variable in this example is healthy growth, which depends on light being present. Light is the independent variable. It doesn't depend on anything.

After the data are collected, they are analyzed to see if they support or reject the hypothesis. The results of one experiment often lead you to a related question. Or they may send you off in a different direction. Whatever the results, something can be learned from every experiment.

Chapter 1

From Atoms to Compounds

Atoms, molecules, and compounds are the building blocks of matter. Atoms are the smallest particles, and when combined, they make a molecule. Chemistry is based on the atomic theory. It states that all matter (anything that has mass) is made of atoms. The first atomic theory was proposed by Democritus, an early Greek philosopher. He lived from about 460 BCE until about 370 BCE. He believed that matter was made up of indivisible, indestructible particles too small to be seen or felt. He called the particles atoms. In Greek, "atom" means "indivisible." Substances, he argued, differ from one another because their atoms are not the same.

Democritus's theory was very different from modern atomic theory. It was based on intuition and speculation. He had no experimental evidence to support his theory. The idea of doing experiments to test the effects of a theory or hypothesis never entered the minds of early Greek philosophers.

By 1800, chemists knew that certain substances, such as oxygen, hydrogen, iron, copper, and many more, could not be broken down into simpler substances. These were called elements. Chemists devised a shorthand way to represent these elements and their atoms. For example, the element hydrogen (or an atom of hydrogen) was represented by the capital letter H, oxygen by O, carbon by C, and so on. (The symbols of some common elements can be found in Table 1.)

Chemists knew, too, that elements sometimes combine during chemical reactions to form compounds. Compounds, they discovered, could be broken down into the elements of which they were made. According to the atomic theory, atoms of different elements combine to form molecules of compounds. Chemists used the same symbols to represent these compounds or molecules of compounds. For example, common table salt is a compound of the elements sodium (Na) and chlorine (Cl). Therefore, the chemical formula for salt is NaCl. The chemical formula for the compound water is H_2O; the formula for carbon dioxide is CO_2. The subscript 2 means there are two atoms of hydrogen in each molecule of water and two atoms of oxygen in each molecule of carbon dioxide.

1.1 Making a Model of Molecules

THINGS YOU WILL NEED:

- several large, identical paper clips
- paper
- several small, identical steel washers

1. Pour several large, identical paper clips onto a sheet of paper. Let the paper clips represent "atoms" of an "element" that has the symbol C.
2. Pour several small, identical steel washers onto a sheet of paper. Let the washers represent "atoms" of an "element" that has the symbol W. Notice that all the "atoms" of C are identical, as are all the "atoms" of W. But as you can see, atoms of C are different from the atoms of W (Figure 1a).
3. Assume element C reacts with element W to form the compound CW. Join some atoms of C with some atoms of W to form molecules of the compound CW (Figure 1b).

In what ratios, other than 1:1, might atoms of C and W combine?

The Atomic Theory

The modern atomic theory of matter sprang from the mind of John Dalton (1766–1844). Dalton, an English Quaker, was both a chemist and a meteorologist (someone who studies weather). Like Democritus, he believed that atoms are tiny, indivisible, and indestructible. According to his theory, the atoms of any one element are identical. But they differ from the atoms of any other element in properties such as weight. Since atoms are indestructible, there is no change in weight when substances undergo physical or chemical change. Therefore, his theory

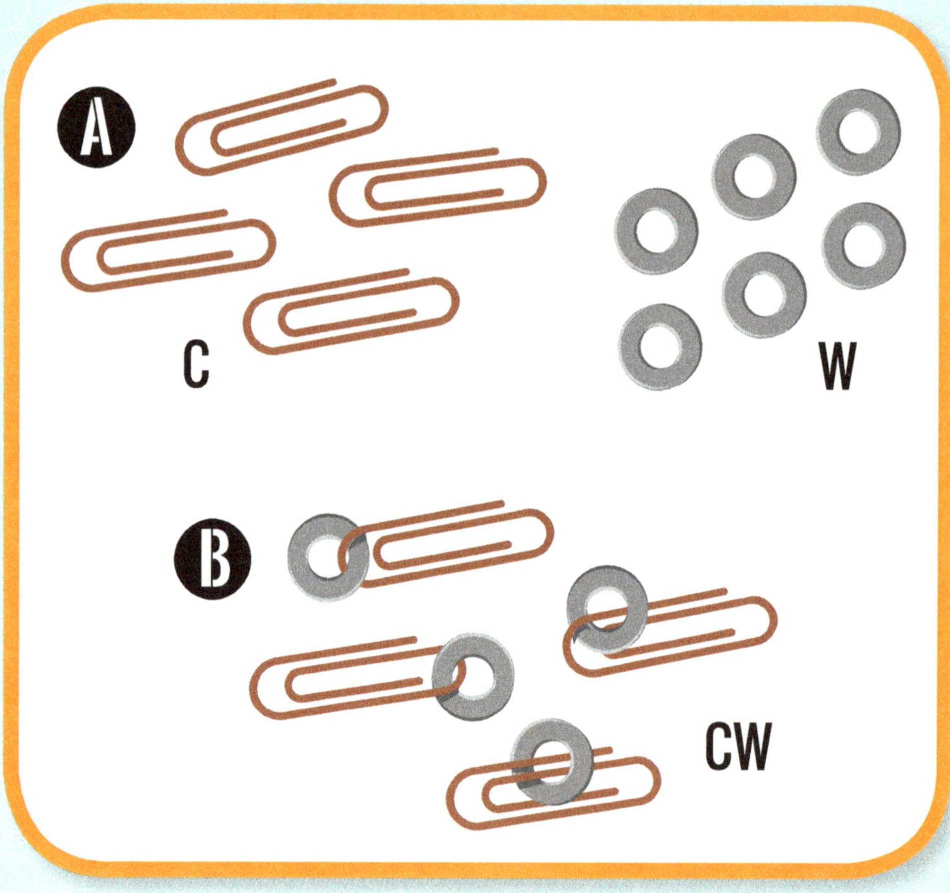

Figure 1. You can make a model of "atoms" of "element C" and "element W" (a) and "molecules" of the "compound CW" (b).

explained a very fundamental law—the law of conservation of matter. The law states that matter is never created nor destroyed. It explains why weight is never lost or gained during chemical reactions or during physical changes such as melting or freezing.

While Dalton's theory of atoms was similar to Democritus's, it differed in a very basic way. Dalton's theory was based on evidence obtained from experiments. Those experiments led to a number of scientific laws. Scientific laws, or laws of nature, are rules about nature for which scientists know no exceptions.

One important law helped lead Dalton to his theory. The law had been discovered by a French chemist, Joseph Louis Proust (1754-1826). Proust had analyzed many compounds and measured the weight of each element in them. His analyses led him to the law of definite proportions. Proust expressed his law in these eloquent words, "We must recognize an invisible hand that holds the balance in the formation of compounds. A compound is a substance to which Nature assigns fixed ratios; it is, in short, a being that Nature never creates other than balance in hand."

In plainer language, when elements combine to form a compound, they combine in a fixed ratio by weight. For example, when oxygen combines with hydrogen to form water, the weight ratio of oxygen to hydrogen is always 8:1. When carbon reacts with oxygen to form carbon dioxide, the ratio of oxygen to carbon by weight is always 2.67:1 or 8:3.

Dalton knew that atoms were far too small to weigh on a balance. But he found ways to measure their weights relative to one another. To find the relative weights of atoms, he separated compounds into their elements. Then he weighed the elements. Or he weighed the elements that combined to form a compound. For example, by passing an electric current through water, he was able to separate water into hydrogen and oxygen. He found that for each 0.80 grams (g) of oxygen collected, he would also collect 0.10 g of hydrogen. If 0.10 g of hydrogen was mixed with 0.80 of oxygen and ignited with a spark, there would be an explosion. After the explosion, there would be no hydrogen or oxygen.

Instead, there would be 0.90 g of water. From this evidence, Dalton concluded that oxygen atoms weigh eight times as much as hydrogen atoms. He assumed that hydrogen and oxygen atoms combine to form water in a ratio of 1:1. Therefore, he concluded, the chemical formula for water was HO.

Later, an Italian chemist, Amedeo Avogadro (1776-1856), hypothesized that equal volumes of gases at the same temperature and pressure contain the same number of molecules. For any volume of oxygen, twice that volume of hydrogen combines with it to form water. If equal volumes are used, half the oxygen remains after the gases combine. Therefore, Avogadro concluded that the formula for water is H_2O, not HO. The subscript 2 indicates that two atoms of hydrogen combine with one atom of oxygen to form one molecule of water. Today we know that Avogadro was right. However, it took half a century before his hypothesis and conclusion about the formula for water was accepted by most chemists.

Since hydrogen is the lightest (least dense) gas known, chemists assigned hydrogen atoms a relative weight of one unit or 1 atomic mass unit (1 amu). No one knew what the actual mass of an atom was. Atoms were too light to be weighed. However, if hydrogen atoms weigh 1 amu, oxygen atoms must weigh 16 amu. Remember, the mass ratio of oxygen to hydrogen in water is 8:1. Remember, too, that the chemical formula for water is H_2O. For both these facts to be true, oxygen atoms must be 16 times as heavy as hydrogen atoms.

$$\frac{\text{Mass of 1 oxygen atom}}{\text{Mass of 2 hydrogen atoms}} = \frac{16\text{ amu}}{2 \times 1\text{ amu}} = \frac{16}{2} = \frac{8}{1} \text{ or } 8{:}1$$

Today we know not only the relative weights of the atoms of every element, we know their actual weights as well. The relative and actual weights of the atoms of some common elements are shown in Table 1.

TABLE 1. Symbols and relative and actual weights of the atoms of some common elements. (Weights are based on oxygen atoms having an atomic weight of 16 amu.)

Element	Symbol	Relative weight of atom in atomic mass units (amu)	Actual weight of atom in septillionths of a gram*
Hydrogen	H	1.0	1.7
Helium	He	4.0	6.7
Carbon	C	12.0	20
Oxygen	O	16.0	27
Sodium	Na	23.0	38.3
Magnesium	Mg	24.3	40.5
Aluminum	Al	27.0	45
Sulfur	S	32.1	53.5
Chlorine	Cl	35.5	59
Iron	Fe	55.8	93
Copper	Cu	63.5	106
Zinc	Zn	65.4	109
Lead	Pb	207	345

*A septillionth of a gram is 0.000000000000000000000001 gram.

1.2 Chemical Formulas

THINGS YOU WILL NEED:

- several large, identical paper clips
- several small, identical steel washers
- balance that can weigh to ± 0.01 g if possible
- notebook
- pen or pencil
- calculator (optional)

In this experiment you will again use large paper clips to represent atoms of element C and small steel washers to represent atoms of element W.

1. Prepare a large number of "molecules" (at least ten) of the compound of CW by joining "atoms" of C and W as shown in Figure 2a. Place all the molecules on a balance pan. Record the weight of the "compound" you have prepared. (If you do not have a balance, assume that atoms of C weigh 1.8 g and that atoms of W weigh 0.6 g.)
2. Next, "decompose" the compound into the elements C and W as shown in Figure 2b. Place the atoms of both elements on the same balance pan you used before. What is the total weight of the elements?
3. Compare the total weight of the two elements with the weight of the compound you prepared. How do your weighings illustrate the law of conservation of matter? That is, how do they illustrate the fact that matter is neither created nor destroyed?
4. Now weigh separately each of the elements that you obtained by decomposing the compound. What is the weight

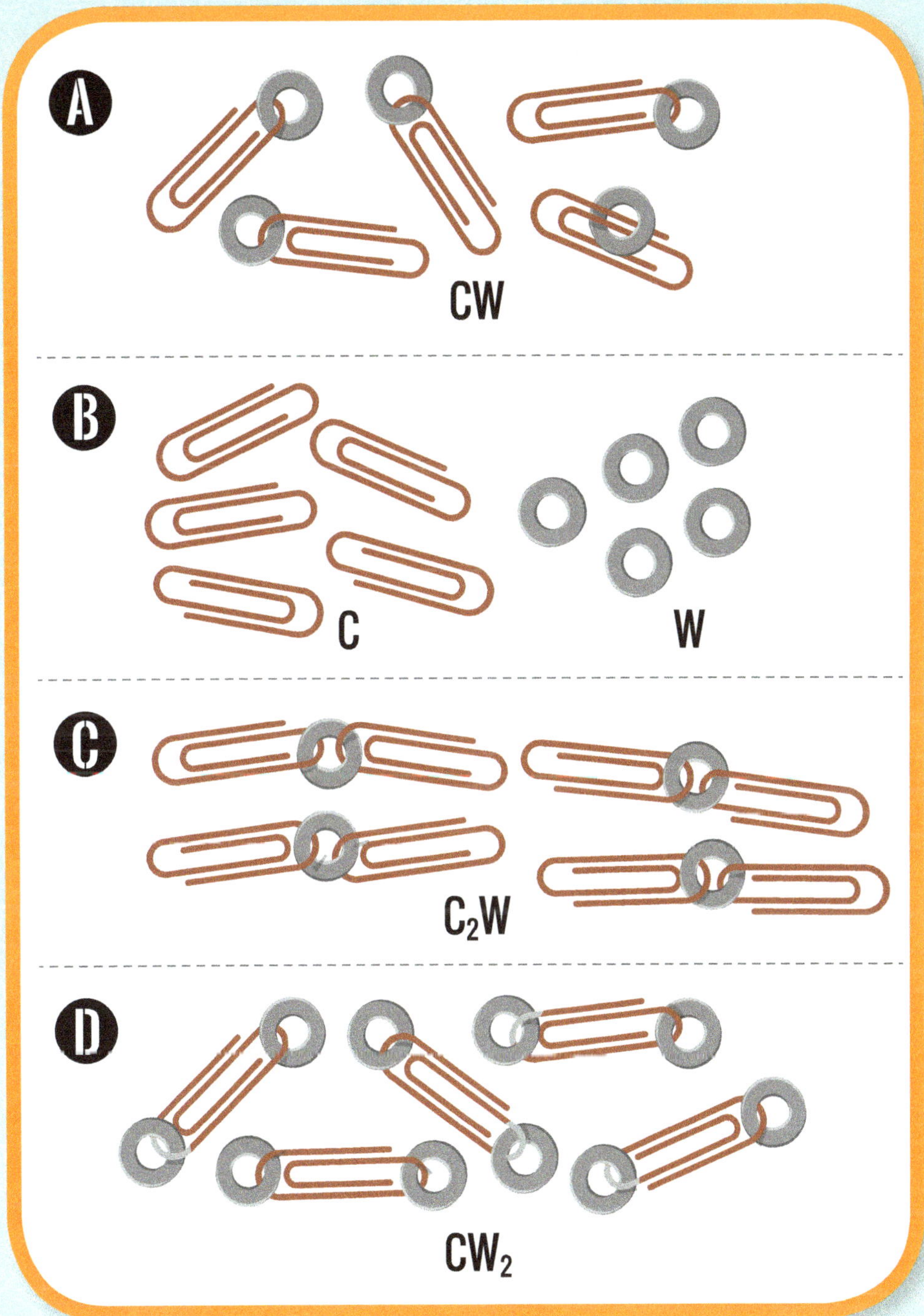

Figure 2. a) "Molecules" of CW b) "Atoms" of the decomposed "compound" CW c) "Molecules" of C_2W d) "Molecules" of CW_2.

of C? What is the weight of W? What is the relative weight of an atom of C to an atom of W? For example, if you found 12 grams of washers had combined with 36 grams of large paper clips, the relative weight of a large paper clip (C) to a washer (W) would be:

$$36/12 = 3/1 \text{ or } 3:1.$$

If the weight of an atom of W is considered to be 10 amu, what is the weight of an atom of C in amu?

5. Repeat the experiment, but prepare only about two-thirds as many molecules of the compound CW. Again, record the weight of the compound. Then decompose the compound into the elements C and W. What was the weight ratio of C to W in the compound?

   How do the results of these two experiments illustrate the law of definite proportions? That is, how do the results demonstrate that elements always combine to form compounds in a fixed ratio by weight?

6. Prepare as many molecules as possible of the compound C_2W (two C atoms and one W atom per molecule). See Figure 2c. The formula C_2W shows that there are two atoms of C and one atom of W in each molecule of C_2W.
7. Place all the molecules of C_2W on a balance pan. Record the weight of the "compound" you have prepared. (If you do not have a balance, assume that atoms of C weigh 1.8 g and that atoms of W weigh 0.6 g.)
8. "Decompose" the compound into the elements C and W. Place the atoms of both elements on the same balance pan you used before. What is the total weight of the elements? Compare the total weight of the two elements with the weight of the compound you prepared.
9. Next, weigh the elements C and W separately. What is the weight ratio of C to W in this compound?

10. Prepare as many molecules as possible of the compound CW_2 (two W atoms and one C atom per molecule). See Figure 2d. The formula CW_2 shows that there are two atoms of W and one atom of C in each molecule of CW_2.
11. Repeat steps 2, 3, and 4 for the compound CW_2.
12. You have now prepared three different compounds of the elements C and W: CW, C_2W, and CW_2. What is the weight ratio of C to W in CW to the ratio of C to W in C_2W? For example, suppose the weight ratio of C to W in CW is 3:1, which is the same as 3; and in C_2W the weight ratio of C to W is 6:1 or 6. Then the weight ratio of C to W in CW to the ratio of C to W in C_2W is 3:6, or 1:2, or 0.5.

    What is the weight ratio of C to W in CW to the ratio of C to W in CW_2?

Law of Multiple Proportions

You have just discovered the law of multiple proportions, another discovery that led Dalton to the atomic theory. The law of multiple proportions states that if two elements form more than one compound, the weight ratio of the elements in one compound will be a simple multiple of the weight ratio in the other compound or compounds.

For example, chemists found that carbon and oxygen combine to form two different gases. In one (carbon monoxide), the weight ratio of oxygen to carbon is 4:3; in the other (carbon dioxide), the ratio is 8:3. The weight ratio of oxygen in carbon dioxide to oxygen in carbon monoxide is 8:4, or more simply 2:1.

Whenever two elements combine to form more than one compound, the law of multiple proportions holds true. As another example, hydrogen and oxygen combine to form two compounds, water (H_2O) and hydrogen peroxide (H_2O_2). As you know, the weight ratio of oxygen to hydrogen in water is 8:1. What is the weight ratio of oxygen to hydrogen in hydrogen peroxide? How do these two compounds illustrate the law of multiple proportions?

Dalton knew that elements sometimes combine to form more than one compound. He had investigated the gaseous compounds formed when nitrogen and oxygen combine. Results similar to his are found in Table 2.

TABLE 2:
Compounds of nitrogen and oxygen

Compound		Weight (w) of oxygen united with 10 g of nitrogen	Weight ratios w:w_3
Name	Chemical formula		
Nitrogen oxide	NO	$w_1 = 11.43$ g	$w_1:w_3 = 11.43: 5.72 = 2:1$
Nitrogen dioxide	NO_2	$w_2 = 22.86$ g	$w_2:w_3 = 22.86: 5.72 = 4:1$
Dinitrogen oxide	N_2O	$w_3 = 5.72$ g	———
Dinitrogen trioxide	N_2O_3	$w_4 = 17.15$ g	$w_4:w_3 = 17.15: 5.72 = 3:1$

Examine the third column of Table 2. It shows the weight of oxygen in each compound that combines with 10 g of nitrogen. Examine the last column of Table 2. It shows the ratio of the weight of oxygen in NO, NO_2, and N_2O_3 to the weight of oxygen in N_2O. N_2O has the least amount of oxygen per 10 g of nitrogen. What would be the weight ratio of $w_2:w_4$? Of $w_2:w_1$?

Evidence for Atoms and Molecules

The laws of definite proportions and multiple proportions can best be explained by assuming three things:

(1) Matter is made up of atoms.

(2) The atoms of an element are identical.

(3) The atoms of an element are different from the atoms of any other element, especially in weight.

There is much more evidence to support the atomic theory. You will examine some of that evidence in the next three experiments.

1.3 Molecules and Brownian Motion

THINGS YOU WILL NEED:

- **an adult**
- Brownian motion apparatus shown in Figure 3 (borrow from your school's science department)
- microscope
- candle
- matches
- a partner
- flashlight

Robert Brown (1773-1858), a Scottish botanist, recognized the importance of the sphere-like structure found in many cells. He gave it its name—nucleus. (Later, you will learn that atoms have nuclei. However, an atom's nucleus is very different from the nucleus of a living cell.)

In 1827, Brown discovered a phenomenon no one could explain. He had prepared a microscope slide by placing some flower pollen in a drop of water. He examined the pollen under a microscope. The pollen grains were being jiggled by some unknown force. A generation passed before anyone could explain this phenomenon, which came to be known as Brownian motion.

By the 1860s, Brownian motion had been explained by Scottish physicists William Thomson (1824-1907), also known as Lord Kelvin, James Clerk Maxwell (1831-1879), and German physicist Ludwig Boltzmann (1844-1906). The pollen particles jiggled because they were being hit repeatedly by fast-moving molecules.

1. You can see Brownian motion for yourself. Borrow a Brownian motion apparatus (Figure 3) from your school's science department. You will also need to borrow a microscope if you do not have one.

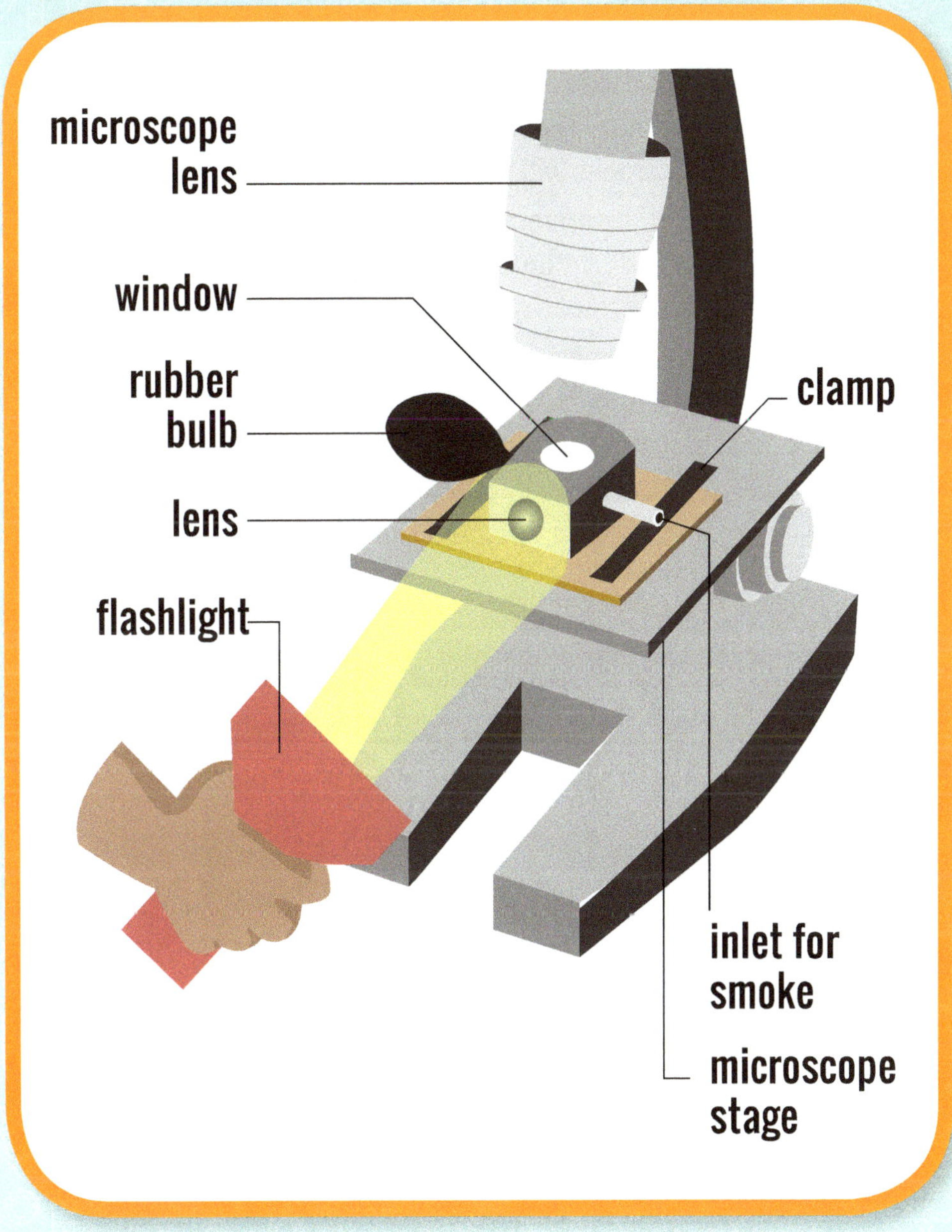

Figure 3. A Brownian motion apparatus will let you see smoke particles being jiggled by speedy molecules of air.

2. **Ask an adult** to light a candle. Once the candle is burning well, **ask the adult** to blow it out. Immediately squeeze the rubber bulb located on one side of the Brownian motion apparatus. Hold the inlet tube in the smoke from the blown-out candle. Then release the bulb. Smoke will be pulled into the viewing chamber.
3. Clamp the base of the apparatus to a microscope stage. Have a partner shine a flashlight onto the lens of the apparatus. The light will reflect from the smoke particles.
4. Look through the microscope's low-power lens (50 or 100) over the window of the apparatus. The smoke particles will appear as bright points of light. Notice how they jiggle as they are hit by fast-moving molecules of air.

IDEA FOR A SCIENCE FAIR PROJECT

- **Obtain some pollen and see if you can make the same observation that Brown made. What other particles can you use to observe Brownian motion?**

1.4 Molecular Motion and Diffusion

THINGS YOU WILL NEED:

- green or blue food coloring
- drinking glass
- cold water
- sugar
- spoons
- warm water
- kitchen baster
- eyedropper
- cooking oil
- quiet place

In this experiment you will find additional evidence that molecules are in constant motion.

1. Add a drop of food coloring to a glass of cold water. Notice how the food coloring slowly spreads through the water. The slow movement of one substance into another is called diffusion.
2. Prepare a saturated solution of sugar. To do this, add a spoonful of sugar to a glass that is about one-third full of warm water. Stir with a spoon. Continue to add sugar and stir until no more sugar will dissolve (disappear) in the water. A small amount of sugar will remain on the bottom of the glass.
3. Add a few drops of blue or green food coloring to the sugar water and stir.
4. Add cold water to a clear glass or plastic cup until it is half full.
5. Squeeze the bulb of a kitchen baster and place the baster's nozzle at the bottom of the colored sugar water. Slowly release the bulb to draw the colored liquid into the baster.

6. Remove the baster from the glass. Carefully lower the baster's nozzle to the bottom of the glass of cold water. Very slowly squeeze the bulb to form a colored layer under the clear water. See Figure 4a. Keep the bulb squeezed as you slowly remove the baster from the water. You should now have a distinct colored layer under the clear water.
7. Use an eyedropper to carefully place a layer of cooking oil on top of the cold water (Figure 4b). You should now have three distinct layers: cooking oil, clear water, and colored sugar water.
8. Carefully move the glass containing the three layers to a quiet place where it will not be disturbed.

Figure 4. **An experiment shows diffusion.**

9. Observe the layers each day. What do you notice? What evidence do you have that molecules of sugar are diffusing into the clear water? Why do you think the diffusion does not extend into the cooking oil?
10. Add cooking oil, water, and a few drops of food coloring to a jar. Seal the jar and shake it. Watch for several minutes. What happens?

For a Science Fair Project IDEA

- **Measure the density (weight per volume) of the water, sugar water, and cooking oil to explain the positions of the three colored layers.**

1.5 Estimating the Size of a Molecule

THINGS YOU WILL NEED:

- water
- clean, large, flat tray, such as the kind found in cafeterias
- ruler
- chalk dust from blackboard eraser
- fine piece of wire
- clothespin
- alcohol
- oleic acid (borrow from school science department or order from science supply company; see appendix)
- a partner
- magnifier

Molecules are very small, but it is possible to estimate their size. You have probably seen the rainbow-colored film that forms when a thin layer of motor oil floats on a puddle of water. Substances insoluble in and less dense than water, such as oil, will float on water. They spread out into a very thin layer on the water's surface. One such substance is oleic acid. It spreads out until it is a layer one or two molecules thick. By finding the thickness of the oleic acid layer, you can estimate the size of its molecules.

1. Pour water onto a very clean, large, flat tray, such as the kind found in cafeterias. The water should be about one centimeter (1/2 inch) deep. When the water is still, sprinkle some powdery chalk dust on its surface. This can be done by tapping a well-used blackboard eraser above the water.
2. Bend a fine piece of wire into a narrow V-shape (Figure 5a). Wind the ends of the wire together and clamp them with a clothespin. Dip the V-shaped part of the wire into some alcohol to clean it.

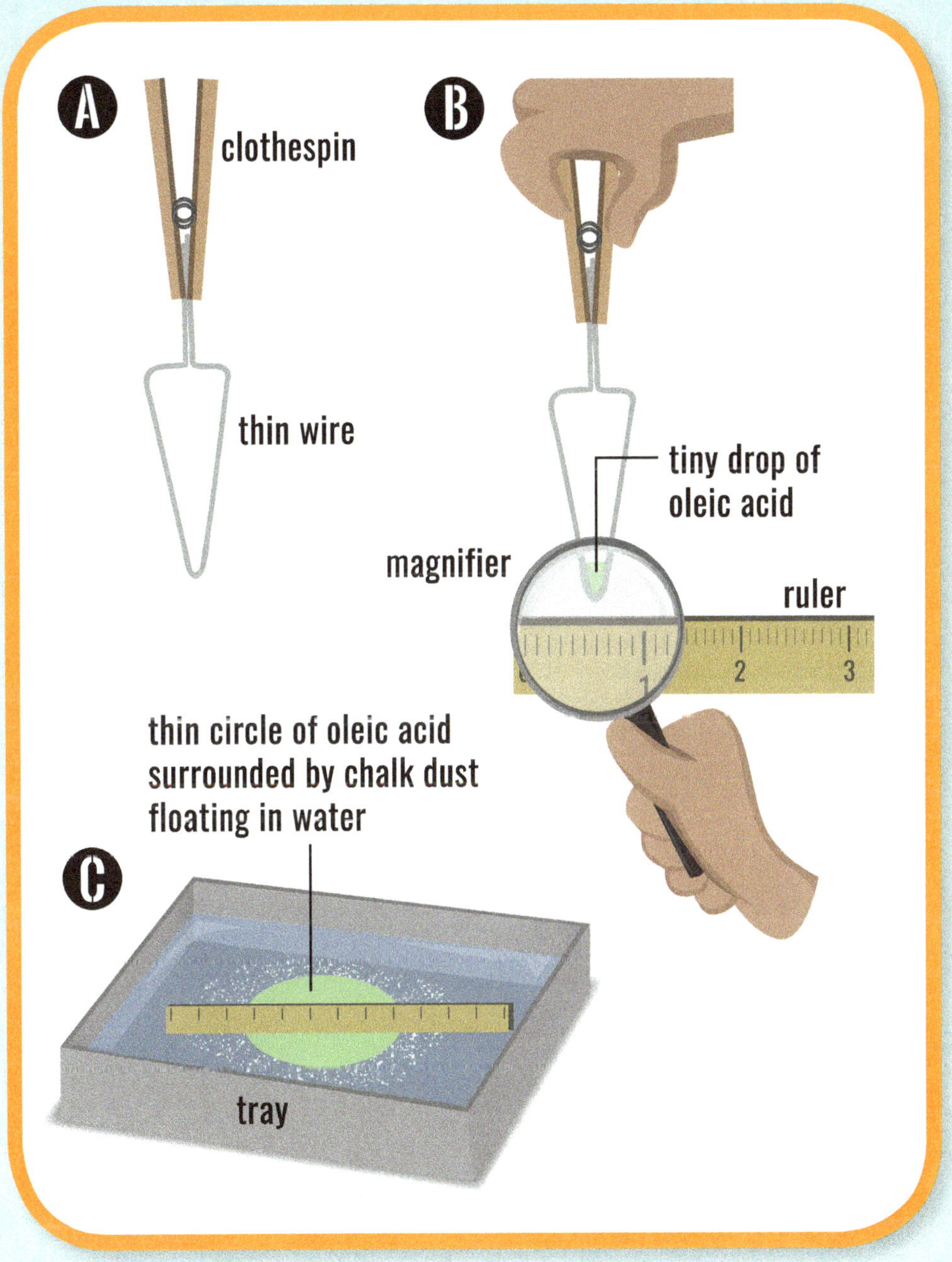

Figure 5. a) A thin V-shaped wire can be held by a clothespin. b) A tiny drop of oleic acid can be measured. c) The drop spreads out on water covered with chalk dust. The diameter of the circle is measured as part of the process to find the size of an oleic acid molecule.

3. When the wire dries, dip the very tip of the V into oleic acid (a liquid). Only a tiny drop will cling to the wire.
4. Estimate the drop's volume. Ask a partner to hold the clothespin. Using a magnifier and a ruler, estimate the diameter of the drop. See Figure 5b.
5. Use your measurement to find the drop's volume. Make the math simple. Assume the drop is a cube. Then simply multiply the diameter (d) by itself twice ($d \times d \times d$). What is your estimate of the drop's volume?
6. Dip the tip of the wire into the center of the water in the tray several times. The drop of oleic acid will spread. It will push the fine powder outward forming a clear circle. The circle is a thin layer of oleic acid. Dip the wire tip into the water several times to be sure all the oleic acid is on the water. Assume that the layer is one molecule thick.
7. Measure the average diameter of the circular layer of oleic acid (Figure 5c). Then calculate the area covered by the oleic acid. Remember, the area of a circle is πr^2. You probably know that π (pi) is approximately 3.14. The thickness (t) of the oleic acid times its area is equal to its volume:

$$t \times \pi r^2 = \text{volume}$$

To find the thickness, divide the volume by the area:

$$t = \frac{\text{volume}}{\pi r^2}$$

The thickness is very small. For example, suppose the diameter of the drop is 0.5 mm and the diameter of the circle of oleic acid is 20 cm. The radius of the circle is 10 cm. The volume of the drop is approximately:

$$0.5 \text{ mm} \times 0.5 \text{ mm} \times 0.5 \text{ mm} = 0.125 \text{ cubic millimeters (mm}^3\text{)}$$

The area covered by the oleic acid is:

$$\pi r^2 = 3.14 \times 10 \text{ cm} \times 10 \text{ cm} = 314 \text{ cm}^2$$

Then the thickness of the layer of oleic acid is:

$$t = \frac{\text{volume}}{\text{area}} = \frac{0.125 \text{ mm}^3}{314 \text{ cm}^2}$$

We cannot divide mm^3 by cm^2, so we need to change square centimeters to square millimeters. Since 1 cm = 10 mm, one square centimeter equals 10 mm × 10 mm = 100 mm^2. Now we can calculate the thickness of the oleic acid.

$$t = \frac{0.125 \text{ mm}^3}{31{,}400 \text{ mm}^2} = 0.000004 \text{ mm or 4 millionths of a millimeter}$$

Using your measurements, what do you estimate the size of a molecule of oleic acid to be?

Inside Atoms

Today, we know much more about atoms, so we have modified Dalton's theory. We know that most of an atom is empty space. Practically all its weight is in a tiny nucleus at the center of the atom. The nucleus contains protons and neutrons. Each proton has a positive electrical charge of -1. The neutrons have no charge but are similar in weight to the protons (about 1.7 septillionths of a gram or 0.00000000000000000000 00017 g).

The charge on each proton is balanced by an equal number of electrons that surround the nucleus. Each electron carries an electrical charge of -1. An electron weighs only 1/2000 as much as a proton. Since the number of electrons in an atom equals the number of protons, the overall charge on an atom is zero. The diagrams in Figure 6a represent the structure of the atoms of a few elements. As you can see, the atoms of each element are different.

Atoms sometimes gain or lose electrons as they join atoms of a different element to form a compound. If an atom loses one electron, it then has one more proton than it has electrons. It will have a charge of +1. Should an atom gain an electron, it will have a charge of -1. Atoms that

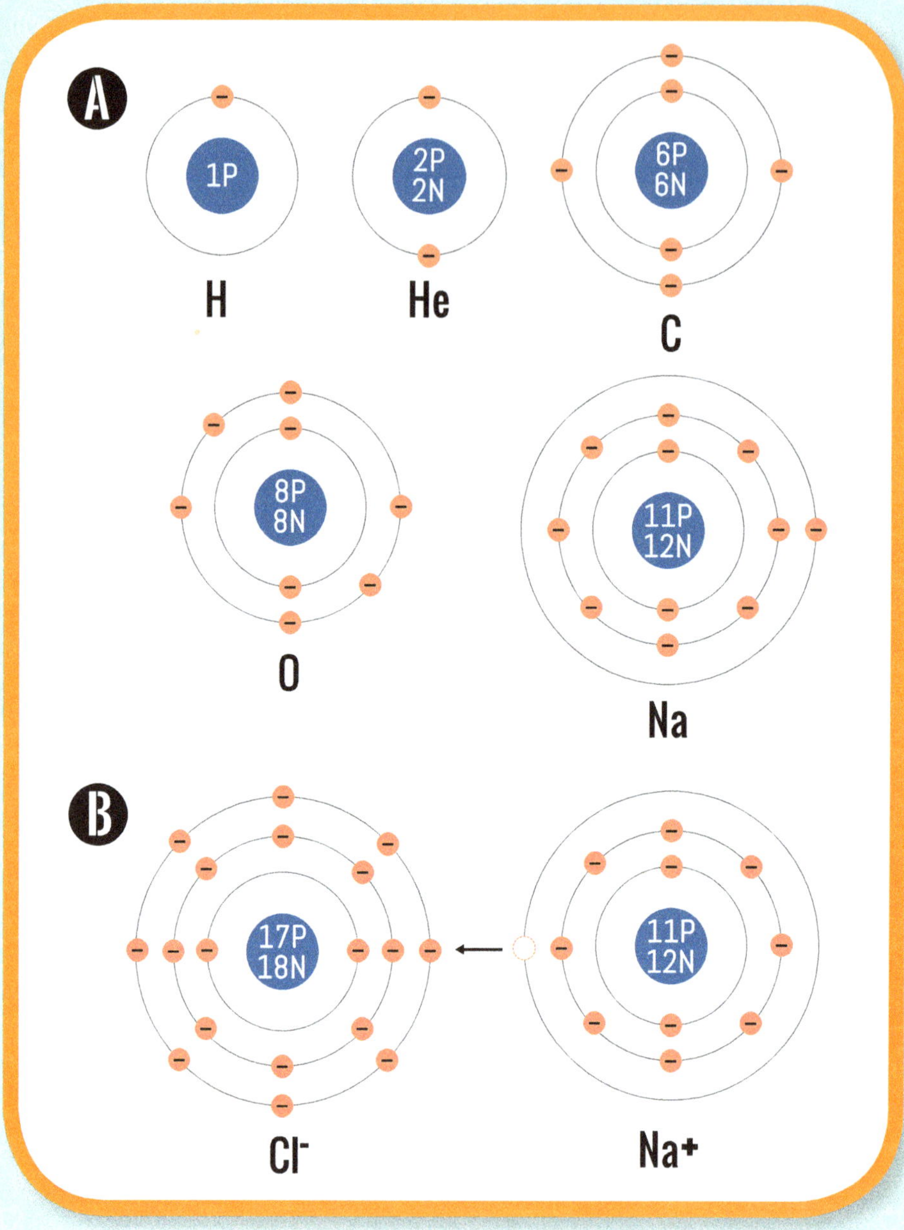

Figure 6. a) The structure of the atoms of several elements are shown. Notice that the number of protons and electrons in an atom are equal. Notice, too, that the electrons of an atom orbit the nucleus at different distances. A maximum of two electrons are found in the first orbit, eight in the next orbit, and more than eight are possible in other orbits. b) If a sodium atom transfers its outermost electron to a chlorine atom, two ions are formed—a sodium ion (Na^+) and a chloride ion (Cl^-)—the ions found in table salt.

carry a charge are called ions. For example, a sodium atom (Na), shown in Figure 6b, might lose the electron to an atom of a different element. It would become a sodium ion (Na^+). If a chlorine atom gained the electron, it would become a negatively charged chloride ion (Cl^-). The result would be sodium chloride (NaCl), the compound we commonly call salt. Compounds formed in this way are said to be bonded ionically.

Compounds can also form when atoms share electrons. The bonding in such compounds is called covalent.

We have had to modify Dalton's theory in other ways as well. We now know that all the atoms of an element are not exactly the same. While all the atoms of a given element have the same number of protons and electrons, the number of neutrons may not be the same. For example, the nuclei of most hydrogen atoms have a single proton and no neutrons. However, a small percentage of hydrogen atoms have one neutron as well as a proton. They weigh twice as much as an ordinary hydrogen atom. An even smaller number of hydrogen atoms have two neutrons and, therefore, weigh three times as much as most hydrogen atoms. Atoms of the same element that differ in the number of neutrons in their nuclei are called isotopes. Hydrogen has three isotopes, and so do oxygen, carbon, and sodium. Helium has only two isotopes, but calcium has eight, as does iron.

Chapter 2

A Look at Chemical Reactions

What happens when water freezes? Is the ice that forms during this physical change still water, or is it a new substance? Physical changes such as freezing, boiling, and evaporating do not result in new substances. Ice is still water when it melts. Chemical changes, however, cause the formation of at least one new substance. Atoms are rearranged, new molecules are formed, and energy is usually absorbed or released.

There are several ways to tell that a chemical reaction is taking place. A gas may be produced. If the gas is formed in a liquid, there will be bubbles and, perhaps, fizzing. A solid (precipitate), sometimes colored, may form and settle out of a liquid. Heat and light may be released as happens when something burns. Reactions that produce heat are called exothermic reactions. There may be a drop in temperature as reactants (the substances that react) form products (new substances) if energy is absorbed. Reactions accompanied by a drop in temperature are said to be endothermic. Other chemical reactions are accompanied by color changes or changes in acidity.

Acids, Bases, and pH

One common chemical reaction is that of an acid with a base. But to understand an acid-base reaction you must first understand acidity and pH. The Latin word for acid, *acidus*, means "sharp" or "sour." It was because of their sour taste that some substances came to be known as acids. In addition to tasting sour, acids dissolve in water to form solutions that conduct electricity. Acids contain hydrogen. That gas is released when the acid is added to certain metals such as zinc. Acids turn blue litmus paper red and they neutralize bases.

Bases are also called alkalis, a word that means "ashes." A harsh soap can be made by boiling wood ashes with animal fat. Bases have a bitter taste and feel slippery like soap. Bases, like acids, conduct electricity. They turn red litmus paper blue and neutralize acids.

When acids and bases combine and neutralize one another, they form water and a salt.

An acid's acidity is due to hydrogen ions it releases in water. Hydrogen ions (H^+) are hydrogen atoms that have lost an electron. A strong acid, such as hydrochloric acid (HCl), a compound of hydrogen and chlorine, forms ions in water. We say it ionizes. We can show that as a chemical equation. The molecules of hydrogen chloride (HCl) ionize (change to ions) in water and become hydrogen ions (H^+) and chloride ions (Cl^-).

$$HCl \rightarrow H^+ + Cl^-$$

Chemists believe that water molecules are involved. The hydrogen ions combine with water molecules to form hydronium ions (H_3O^+).

$$H^+ + H_2O \rightarrow H_3O^+$$

An acid's strength depends on how many hydronium ions it forms in water. It is the presence of the ions that makes acids conductors of electricity.

Bases form hydroxide ions (OH^-) in water. For example, sodium hydroxide (NaOH), also known as lye, is made up of sodium ions (Na^+) and hydroxide ions. These ions separate in water as shown by the following equation:

$$NaOH \rightarrow Na^+ + OH^-$$

The strength of an acid or base can be determined by its pH—a measure of the concentration of hydrogen ions. The pH scale was devised in 1909 by the Danish chemist Søren Peter Lauritz Sørensen (1868–1939). Neutral substances (neither acidic nor basic) have a pH of 7. Substances with a pH less than 7 are acidic; substances with a pH greater than 7 are basic. An acid with a pH of 1 is very acidic; one with a pH of 3 to 5 is mildly acidic. A solution with a pH of 14 is very basic; one with a pH of 9 to 11 is mildly basic.

1	2	3	4	5	6	7	8	9	10	11	12	13	14
strong acid			mild acid			neutral			mild base			strong base	

Litmus paper can determine whether a substance is an acid or a base. However, litmus paper alone cannot measure pH. Fortunately, there are acid-base indicators that change color at different concentrations of hydrogen ions. Several such indicators are blended in pH paper, which can be used to measure pH over a range of 1 to 14.

2.1 The pH of Acids and Bases

THINGS YOU WILL NEED:

- pickle juice
- pH paper (roll or individual strips) with color scale
- teaspoon
- baking soda (sodium bicarbonate)
- water
- medicine cups or small vials
- powdered dishwasher detergent (sodium carbonate)
- notebook
- pen or pencil
- white vinegar
- lemon juice
- tomato juice
- orange juice
- milk
- soap
- ammonia (household)
- saliva

1. Taste a few drops of pickle juice. (It is safe to taste pickle juice.) Do you think it is an acid or a base? Test your prediction. Dip a strip of pH paper into the pickle juice. Compare the color of the wet strip with the color chart on the pH paper container. Was your prediction correct? Do not use a strip of pH paper more than once.
2. Mix a teaspoon of baking soda with a small amount of water in a medicine cup or small vial. Do the same with powdered dishwasher detergent. Use pH paper to determine the pH of both.
3. Pour some white vinegar into a medicine cup or vial. Dip one end of a strip of pH paper into the vinegar. What is the pH of vinegar? Record that pH in your notebook.

4. Pour some white vinegar into a medicine cup or vial. Dip one end of a strip of pH paper into the vinegar. What is the pH of vinegar? Record that pH in your notebook.
5. Repeat the procedure for each of the other substances. Which substance was the most acidic (lowest pH)? Which substance was least acidic (highest pH)? Which substances were acids? Which substances were bases?
6. A substance with a pH of 3 is only one hundredth (1/100) as acidic as a substance with a pH of 1. To see that this is true, measure the pH of 1 mL of lemon juice. Dilute the 1 mL by adding 99 mL of water. What pH can you expect after adding 99 mL of water to 1 mL of lemon juice? Measure the pH. Were you right?

For a Science Fair Project: IDEAS

- **Prepare a cup of hot tea. Add a few drops of lemon juice. What evidence do you have that tea is an acid-base indicator?**
- **See if you can extract dyes from garden flowers. How do these colors respond to acids and bases?**
- **Investigate other common indicators. Indicators can be found in many school science rooms or obtained from a science supply company (see appendix). These include phenolphthalein, methyl orange, methyl red, bromthymol blue, congo red, indigo carmine, and alizarin yellow. Other than color, how do they differ?**

2.2 Acid and Base Models

THINGS YOU WILL NEED:

- gumdrops of three different colors
- toothpicks

You can make models to help you better understand acids and bases. The models can be made from gumdrops of several different colors. Tooth picks can represent the chemical bonds that hold the atoms in molecules together.

1. Prepare a molecule of hydrogen chloride (HCl). Use a gumdrop of one color, say yellow, for the chlorine atom and a different colored gumdrop, say red, for the hydrogen atom. Connect the two atoms with a toothpick (see Figure 7a).
2. Prepare a model of a water molecule from three gumdrops. The oxygen should have a different color than the hydrogen and chlorine. In Figure 7b, the oxygen atom is white and the two hydrogen atoms are red. Notice that the two hydrogens are at an angle of approximately 100 degrees, not 180 degrees. In real water molecules, we know the two hydrogens are 104 degrees apart.
3. Separate the hydrogen chloride molecule into hydrogen and chloride ions. [Assume the hydrogen donates its electron to the chlorine atom to form a hydrogen ion (H+) and a chloride ion (Cl^-).] See Figure 7c.
4. Use a toothpick to join the hydrogen ion to the water molecule to form the hydronium ion (Figure 7d).
5. Join an oxygen atom and a hydrogen atom to form the hydroxide ion (OH^-). See Figure 7e.

6. Place the hydronium ion (H_3O^+) model and the hydroxide ion model next to one another (Figure 7f). What do you think might happen if these two ions were to collide with one another?

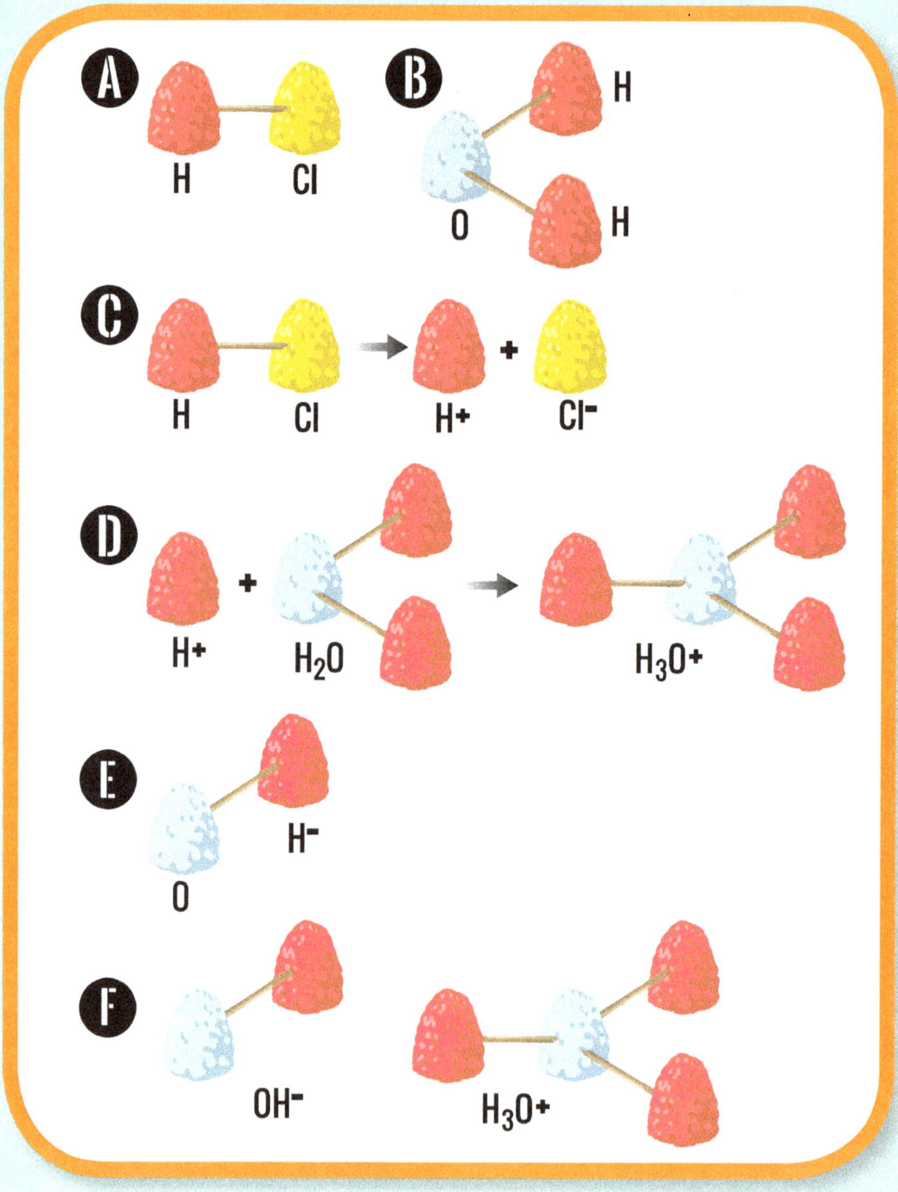

Figure 7. **Models show the atoms, ions, and molecules that form acids and bases.**

2.3 Neutralization Reactions

THINGS YOU WILL NEED:

- unsweetened grape juice
- eyedropper
- medicine cups or clear vials
- vinegar
- household ammonia
- teaspoon
- milk of magnesia
- saucer
- water
- lemon juice

Seeing the hydronium and hydroxide ions side by side may have led you to guess that they might combine to form water. If you did, you guessed correctly. Acids and bases do combine to form water. The reaction is called neutralization, and the products are water and a salt. For example, hydrochloric acid and sodium hydroxide combine to form water and sodium chloride (table salt).

$$HCl + NaOH \rightarrow H_2O + NaCl$$

In this experiment you will use a natural indicator (unsweetened grape juice) as your acid-base indicator.

1. Use an eyedropper to add 10 drops of the grape juice to each of two medicine cups or clear vials. Add vinegar (acetic acid) to one cup. Add ammonia to the other cup. What is the color of grape juice in an acid? In a base?
2. Pour about 1/2 teaspoon of milk of magnesia [$Mg(OH)_2$] into a saucer. Add 2 teaspoons of water and stir. Add 10 drops of the grape juice to the milk of magnesia solution.
3. Add lemon juice drop by drop to the milk of magnesia. Stir thoroughly after each addition. At some point, the color of the solution will change. You have just gone beyond the point of neutralization.

4. Now go the other way. Rinse your eyedropper and use it to add drops of milk of magnesia to the solution.

IDEAS FOR A SCIENCE FAIR PROJECT

- Antacids are sold as tablets or liquids. They are used to neutralize stomach acid. Design and carry out, **under adult supervision**, an experiment to test various antacids for their capacity to neutralize acids. Examine the list of ingredients in the antacid. Can you figure out how the antacid neutralizes the acid?
- Does cooking change the pH of onion juice?

2.4 Conducting Electricity

THINGS YOU WILL NEED:

- paper clips
- plastic medicine cup
- vinegar
- 3 flexible wires with alligator clips
- 6-volt lantern battery
- galvanometer or milliammeter
- household ammonia

As you have seen, acids and bases form ions in water (H_3O^+ and OH^-). Since ions are atoms that carry an electric charge, you might expect that acids and bases will conduct electricity. You can do an experiment to find out.

To avoid the danger of strong acids or bases, you will use vinegar (acetic acid), a weak acid, and ammonia, a weak base.

1. Slide a paper clip over the side of a plastic medicine cup. Half the paper clip should be inside the cup. Slide a second paper clip over the opposite side of the cup.
2. Nearly fill the cup with vinegar (acetic acid). Using flexible wires with alligator clips, make the connections shown in Figure 8. Use a wire to connect one paper clip to the positive pole of a 6-volt lantern battery. Connect the other paper clip to the positive pole of a galvanometer or milliammeter. Use a third wire to connect the negative pole of the battery to the negative pole of the galvanometer or milliammeter. Such meters can measure thousandths of an ampere. An ampere is the unit used to measure electric current (a flow of electrons).

   Does the meter indicate an electric current? If it does, how large is the current? For comparison, a AAA cell alone can produce a current of 3 amperes.

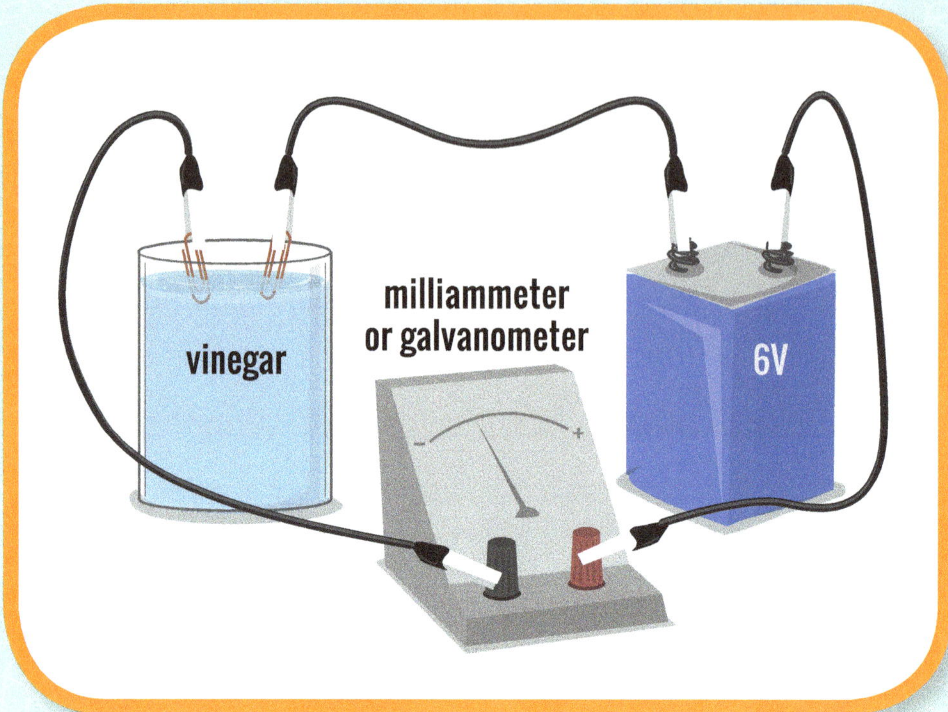

Figure 8. **Acids can conduct electricity.**

3. Repeat the experiment using a solution of household ammonia in place of the vinegar.

   Does the meter indicate an electric current? If it does, how large is the current?

   What current do you think would be produced if you used a strong acid or a strong base? Under the supervision of a chemistry teacher, you might test your prediction.

2.5 A Bubbling Reaction

THINGS YOU WILL NEED:

- **an adult**
- graduated cylinder or metric measuring cup
- vinegar
- flask or small bottle
- funnel
- balloon
- teaspoon
- baking soda
- clay
- wide jar or glass
- birthday candle
- matches

What happens when baking soda [sodium bicarbonate ($NaHCO_3$)] and vinegar [acetic acid ($C_2H_4O_2$)] come together? You can find out!

1. Pour about 50 mL of vinegar into a flask or small bottle.
2. Place a funnel in the mouth of a balloon (Figure 9a). Using the funnel, pour one teaspoon of baking soda into the balloon. Tap the funnel to be sure all the baking soda gets into the balloon.
3. Pull the neck of the balloon over the top of the flask or bottle that contains the vinegar. Then lift the balloon as shown in Figure 9b so that the baking soda falls into the vinegar. What indicates that a chemical reaction is taking place?

   Let the reaction continue until the bubbling stops.

   From the chemical formulas $NaHCO_3$ and $C_2H_4O_2$, you can see that the gas in the balloon might be one of several gases. It could be oxygen (O_2), which makes things burn faster; hydrogen (H_2), which burns; or carbon dioxide (CO_2), which is used to extinguish fires.

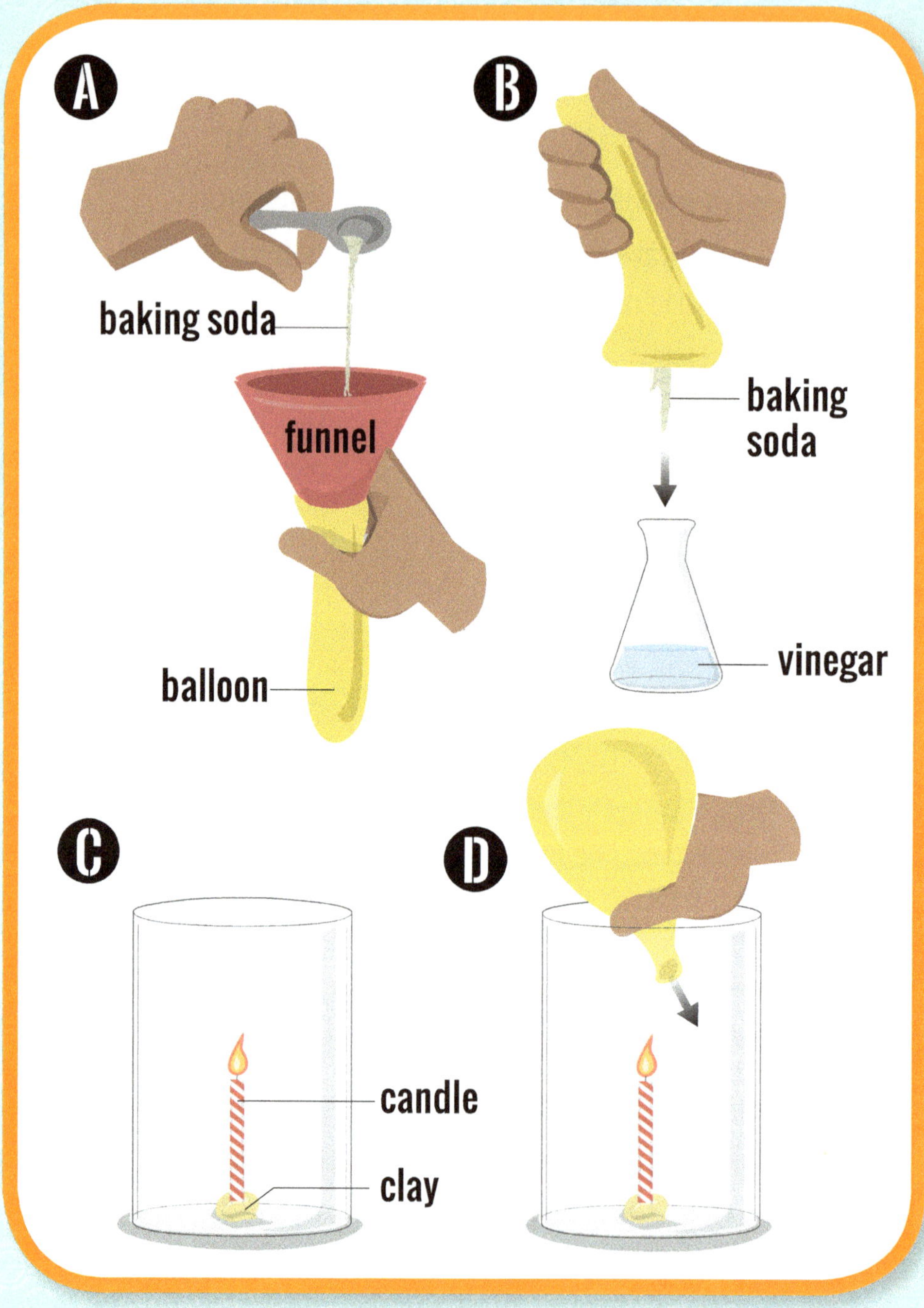

Figure 9. a) Add a teaspoon of baking soda to a balloon. b) Pull the neck of the balloon over a flask or bottle that contains white vinegar. Empty the baking soda into the flask. c) Light a small candle in a wide jar. d) Slowly release the balloonful of gas into the jar that holds the burning candle.

4. To find out which gas it is, place a small lump of clay on the bottom of a wide jar or glass. Use the clay to support an upright birthday candle (Figure 9c). **Ask an adult** to light the candle.
5. Let the candle burn until it is quite short. Be sure the candle flame is well below the top of the jar.
6. Squeeze the neck of the balloon so the gas cannot escape. Then remove the balloon from the flask or bottle. Put the neck of the balloon into the jar with the candle. Slowly release the gas (Figure 9d). What happens to the candle flame? What gas was produced by the reaction of $NaHCO_3$ with $C_2H_4O_2$?

IDEAS FOR A SCIENCE FAIR PROJECT

- How is baking powder different than baking soda? Try adding water to baking powder. What happens? Is the gas the same gas you obtained from baking soda and vinegar?
- Will other acids react with baking soda to produce carbon dioxide? Try lemon juice, orange juice, grapefruit juice, and solutions of citric acid such as Tang and Kool-Aid.
- Is the reaction between vinegar and baking soda exothermic or endothermic? Do an experiment to find out.

2.6 The Rate of Reaction

THINGS YOU WILL NEED:

- seltzer tablets
- water
- ice cubes
- drinking glasses
- cold tap water
- graduated cylinder or metric measuring cup
- hot tap water

Some reactions, such as the explosion of gun powder, go quickly. Other reactions, such as rusting, go slowly. In this experiment, you will see how temperature affects the rate of the reaction between seltzer tablets and water.

1. Examine a package of seltzer tablets to find out what chemicals are in a seltzer tablet. Why do you think there will be a reaction when the tablet is placed in water?
2. Prepare some ice water. Fill a glass two-thirds of the way with cold water. Fill the remaining third with ice cubes.
3. After five minutes, pour 150 mL of the ice water into a glass. Pour 150 mL of hot tap water into a second identical glass.
4. Add one seltzer tablet to the cold water. At the same time, add another seltzer tablet to the hot water. How does temperature affect the speed of a chemical reaction?
5. How does surface area affect the rate of a reaction? To find out, crush a seltzer tablet into tiny pieces. Simultaneously drop the crushed tablet and a whole tablet into equal amounts of cold water in separate identical glasses. What do you conclude?

2.7 One More Chemical Reaction

THINGS YOU WILL NEED:

- steel wool that has no soap (obtain from hardware store)
- a jar
- vinegar
- 2 eyedroppers
- graduated cylinder or metric measuring cup
- 2 medicine cups or clear vials
- household ammonia

1. Soak a pad of soapless steel wool in a jar of vinegar (acetic acid) for twenty-four hours. The iron (Fe) in the steel wool reacts with acetic acid to form ferrous acetate [$Fe(C_2H_3O_2)_2$].
2. Using an eyedropper, remove about 5 mL of iron acetate solution from the jar that contains the steel wool. Put the iron acetate in a medicine cup or clear vial.
3. Pour a little ammonia into a separate medicine cup or vial. Use a second eyedropper to add about 5 mL of the ammonia to the iron acetate. What happens when the two liquids mix? What do you see that indicates a chemical reaction has occurred?
4. Let the medicine cup or vial with the iron acetate sit overnight. What happens to the color of the solid (precipitate) that formed?

2.8 Electrical Energy from a Reaction

THINGS YOU WILL NEED:

- small jar
- water
- teaspoon
- salt
- large galvanized (zinc-coated) nail
- heavy copper wire
- 2 flexible wires with alligator clips
- voltmeter (0–5 or 0–1 volt range)
- galvanometer or milliammeter

1. Nearly fill a small jar with water. Add one or two teaspoons of salt. Stir to dissolve the salt and make a salt solution.
2. Place a large galvanized (zinc-coated) nail in the jar. Place a heavy copper wire on the opposite side of the jar. The nail and wire will serve as electrodes. Make sure the electrodes do not touch one another. Use small pieces of tape to fix the electrodes to the jar (Figure 10a).
3. Use flexible wires with alligator clips to connect the electrodes to a voltmeter. A wire should connect the nail to the negative pole of the voltmeter. A second wire should connect the copper wire to the positive pole of the meter. A voltmeter can measure the energy of any charges that flow between the two electrodes.

   Is there a voltage between the two electrodes? If so, what is it?
4. The electric current between the two electrodes is probably very small. You may be able to measure it with a galvanometer or a milliammeter, which can measure thousandths of an ampere. Were you able to measure an electric current? If so, what was it?

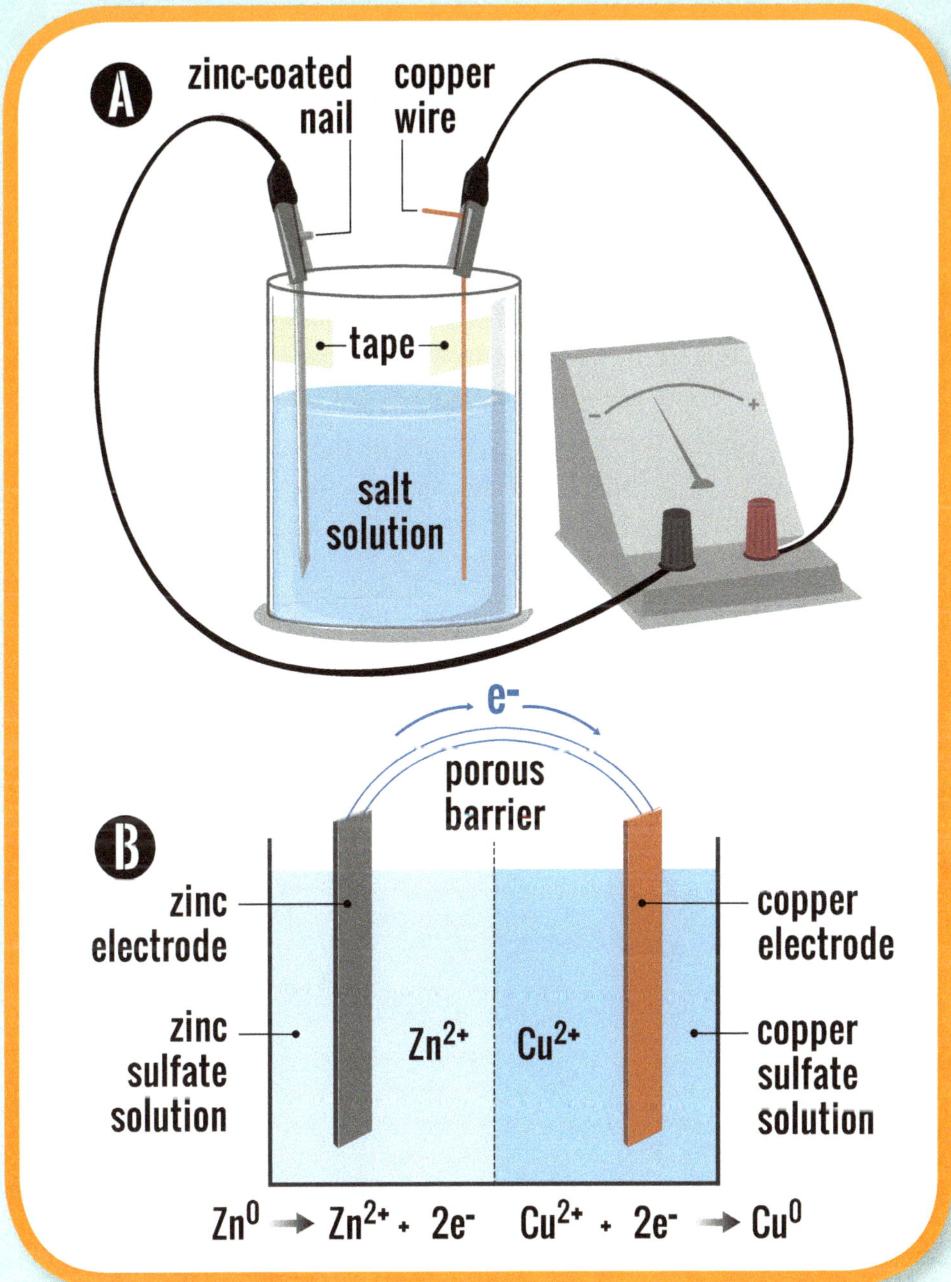

Figure 10. a) In this simple electric cell, chemical energy is changed into electric energy. b) In this electric cell, zinc atoms in the negative electrode give up electrons that travel along a wire to the positive copper electrode. At the copper electrode, copper ions in the solution containing copper ions gain the electrons and become copper atoms that collect on the positive electrode.

Chemicals to Electric Energy

As you have just seen, the energy stored in chemicals can be changed to electrical energy. Zinc will more readily give up electrons than will copper. That is why the zinc electrode was connected to the negative pole of the meter.

In an electric cell like the one shown in Figure 10b, electrons flow from the zinc electrode to the copper electrode. The zinc atoms (Zn) give up two electrons per atom and go into solution as zinc ions (Zn^{2+}). Each copper ion (Cu^{2+}) gains two electrons at the copper electrode. The uncharged atoms (Cu) collect on the copper electrode.

As you will learn in Chapter 3, this reaction is an example of an oxidation-reduction reaction.

Chapter 3

Studying Oxygen and Oxidation

We live on planet Earth, and we breathe air every day. What elements make up much of our air and planet?

Oxygen makes up 21 percent of the air and 46 percent of Earth's crust. Water, which is 89 percent oxygen, covers two-thirds of Earth's surface. Nitrogen, which makes up 78 percent of the air, is nonreactive. Oxygen is very reactive. It combines with a great many elements to form compounds. When it combines with one other element, the compound is called an oxide. Examples of oxides are: carbon monoxide (CO), carbon dioxide (CO_2), calcium oxide (CaO), and aluminum oxide (Al_2O_3). Hydrogen oxide (H_2O) is more commonly called water.

The chemical combination of oxygen with other elements to form compounds is called oxidation. Sometimes oxidation is rapid. Burning wood is an example of rapid oxidation. Sometimes, as when iron turns to iron oxide (rust), oxidation is slow.

3.1 Reactants and Products of Oxidation

THINGS YOU WILL NEED:

- **an adult**
- short candle
- matches
- tin can lid
- ice cubes
- drinking glass
- water
- blue cobalt chloride paper (borrow from school science teacher)
- white china saucer or small dish
- two 250-mL beakers or cup-size drinking glasses
- graduated cylinder or metric measuring cup
- limewater (borrow from school science teacher)
- soda straw

Because you will be using a candle flame in this experiment, you should work with an adult.

A candle consists of wax that surrounds a wick. The wax, an organic (carbon) compound, burns slowly, producing heat and light. Candle wax is a mixture of paraffin, stearic acid, and beeswax. Paraffin is itself a mixture of large molecules that contain only carbon and hydrogen (hydrocarbons). Stearic acid ($C_{18}H_{36}O_2$) comes from animal fat. Beeswax, a mixture of heavy organic molecules, is secreted by bees to make honeycombs.

When a chemical reaction takes place, substances that change during the reaction are called reactants. New substances that form during the reaction are called products. When a candle burns, its organic molecules combine with oxygen and the wax slowly disappears. The reactants of this reaction are candle wax and oxygen. What do you think the products are? Let's find out.

1. **With adult help**, light a candle no taller than 5 cm (2 in). Once the candle is burning smoothly, tip it so that some wax falls onto a tin can lid. Place the candle on the liquid wax. When the wax solidifies, it will keep the candle upright and in place. (See Figure 11a.)
2. Place some ice cubes in a glass and add some water. **Ask an adult** to hold the glass of ice water several inches above the flame as shown in Figure 11b. Notice the clear liquid that condenses on the glass. Does it have a color? Does it have an odor? Normally, you should not taste liquid products, but in this case it is permissible. Put a little of the liquid on your tongue. As you can see, it is colorless, odorless, and tasteless, just like water. Could the condensed liquid be water?
3. If you have blue cobalt paper, use it to test for water. Bluish cobalt chloride turns pink when it touches water. What do you conclude?

   There was carbon in the wax, but water is H_2O, a compound of hydrogen and oxygen. Is there a product that contains carbon?
4. **Ask an adult** to hold a white china saucer or dish in the flame for a few seconds. After the china is removed, look at the deposit on its surface. What color is it? Could it be carbon?
5. **Ask the adult** to hold another china dish several inches above the flame, where the ice water was held. You will find that no black deposit collects on the dish. Perhaps the hot carbon reacts with oxygen to form a gas. We know that carbon burns to form carbon dioxide (CO_2). Let's see if we can detect carbon dioxide.
6. Place a 250-mL beaker or cup-size drinking glass beside the candle. Then invert a second identical beaker or glass over the candle (Figure 11c). After the flame goes out, remove the second beaker or glass. Place it beside the first one. Add 10 mL

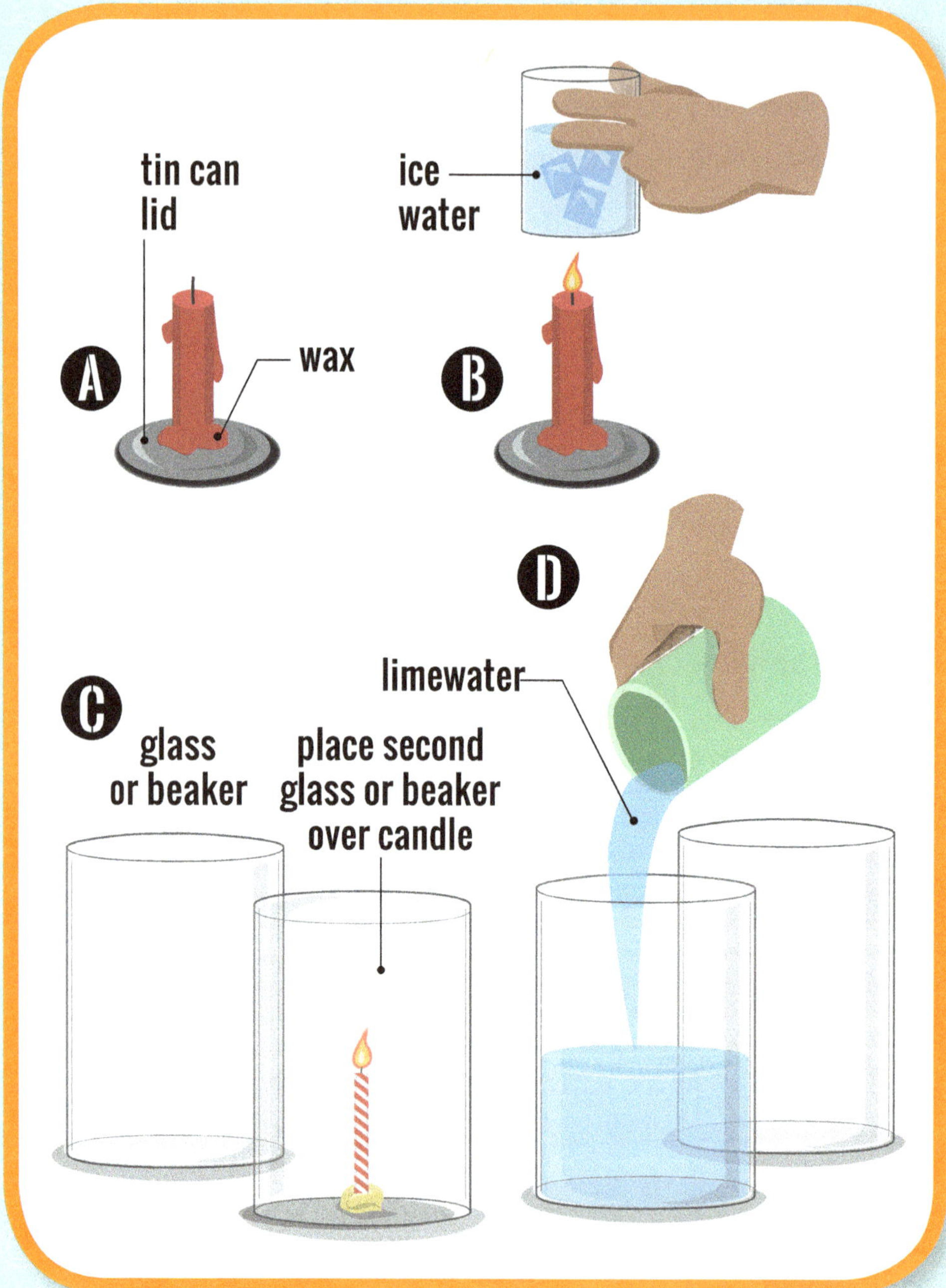

Figure 11. a) Attach a candle to a tin can lid. b) Hold a glass or beaker of ice water above the candle flame. c) Invert a glass or beaker over the burning candle. d) Add limewater to the gas in the glass or beaker.

of limewater to both beakers or glasses and swirl them (Figure 11d). Limewater turns milky in the presence of carbon dioxide (CO_2). Does the limewater in either flask turn milky? What can you conclude?

As you may know, there is carbon dioxide in the air you exhale. Using a soda straw, blow into the limewater in the flask that didn't become milky. What do you predict will happen? Try it! Was your prediction correct? Based on your experiments, what are two likely products of the reaction between candle wax and oxygen?

There are two possible reasons the candle went out when the air supply was limited. One is that one or more of the reactants was in limited supply. The other is that one or more of the products that was not removed stopped the reaction. Why do you think the candle went out when it was covered by a glass vessel?

FOR A SCIENCE FAIR PROJECT IDEA

- What is spontaneous combustion? **Under adult supervision**, design and carry out an experiment to demonstrate spontaneous combustion.

3.2 An Exothermic Chemical Reaction

THINGS YOU WILL NEED:

- **an adult**
- short candle fixed to a tin can lid
- balance to weigh things to ± 0.1 g or better
- notebook
- pen or pencil
- empty large (28-36 oz) can
- can openers
- paper punch
- empty 6-oz frozen juice can with metal base and cardboard sides
- stick, glass rod, or a long nail
- thermometer (-10 to 110°C)
- cold water
- matches

A match was required to light the candle in the previous experiment. The match flame was needed to start the chemical reaction (the burning of the wax). This reaction, like many chemical reactions, requires some energy—the activation energy—to start the reaction. A lighted match provided the activation energy needed to start the candle burning. Once it began, the reaction was exothermic (gave off heat). A burning candle releases heat, so it is an exothermic reaction. The energy changes involved are shown in Figure 12a.

Potential (chemical) energy is stored in the candle. It is released and appears as heat once you provide the activation energy. You can measure the energy released per gram of wax burned.

1. Weigh the short candle fixed to a tin can lid that was used in the previous experiment. Record the weight in your notebook.

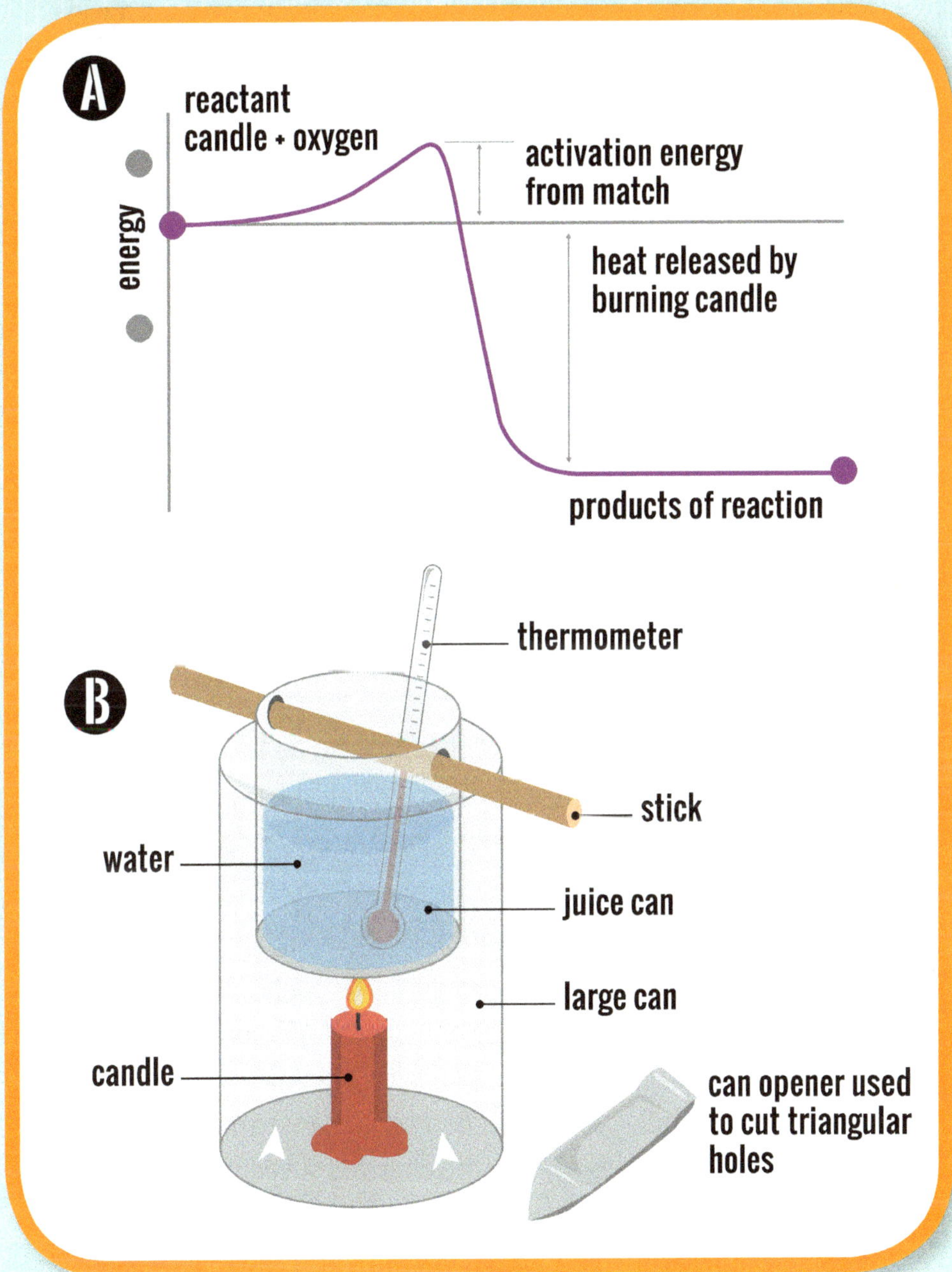

Figure 12. a) The energy involved with a burning candle b) This apparatus can be used to measure the energy released when a candle burns.

2. Remove the bottom of a large (28–36 oz) empty can. Use a can opener to cut 5 or 6 triangular holes around the base of the can.
3. Using a paper punch, make two holes, on opposite sides, near the top of an empty frozen juice can. Put a stick, glass rod, or a long nail through the holes in the can. Then place the small can inside the large can as shown in Figure 12b. The stick, rod, or nail will support the juice can on the larger can. The holes in the bottom of the larger can will allow air to enter the can so the candle will burn after being lit.
4. Lift the large can. Place the candle under the small juice can. Add 100 mL of cold water (10–15°C below room temperature) to the small can. (Since 1 mL of water weighs 1 g, 100 mL of water weigh 100 g.) Use a thermometer to measure the temperature. Record the temperature.
5. Lift the two cans and **ask an adult** to light the candle. Replace the cans over the burning candle. The top of the flame should just touch the bottom of the smaller can that holds the cold water.
6. Stir the water with the thermometer. When the temperature of the water is 10–15°C above room temperature, blow out the candle. Record the final temperature of the water.
7. Weigh the candle and lid. Record the final weight.

A calorie is the heat needed to raise the temperature of one gram of water by one degree Celsius. How much heat, in calories, did the candle transfer to the water? How much weight did the candle lose? How much heat per gram of wax burned is released by this reaction of candle wax with oxygen? Use the data you collected to answer this question.

For example, suppose the temperature of the water rose 25°C, from 10°C to 35°C. In that case, the heat delivered to the water was 2,500 calories because:

$$100\text{g} \times 25°\text{C} = 2{,}500\ \text{cal.}$$

If the candle lost 0.40 grams, the heat per gram released by the burning candle was 6,300 cal/g because:

$$2{,}500 \text{ cal} = \frac{6{,}300 \text{ cal/g}}{0.40 \text{ g}}$$

IDEAS FOR A SCIENCE FAIR PROJECT

- Some of the heat released as the candle burned was not transferred to the water. It was used to warm the surrounding air and the cans. Design a way to do this experiment that would reduce heat loss to the surroundings. Then, **under adult supervision**, carry out the experiment. How much heat per gram of wax burned is produced in this reaction when you use your modified experiment? How does it compare with the value you found before?
- Does the heat per gram of wax burned depend on the kind of candle you burn? Design an experiment to find out. Then, **under adult supervision**, carry out your experiment.
- How much heat is released when a peanut burns? Design an experiment to find out. Then carry out the experiment **under adult supervision**.

Fuel for the Fire

For burning (rapid oxidation) to occur, there must be a fuel (something that will burn), oxygen to support the burning, and the activation energy needed to start the reaction. The activation energy is needed to reach the fuel's ignition temperature—the temperature at which it will burn. As you know, this can often be accomplished with a match, but there are other ways as well.

As any firefighter will tell you, there are several ways to extinguish a fire. (1) Remove the fuel, which is often not possible. (2) Lower the temperature below the ignition temperature. This is sometimes accomplished by pouring water on the fire. (3) Remove the oxygen. This can be accomplished by smothering the fire—enclosing the fuel so that air cannot reach it. A person whose clothes are on fire will often run. This is the worst thing he or she can do. It brings more oxygen to the flames. Instead, the person should roll on the ground or floor to separate the flames from oxygen. Another person can accomplish the same thing even more effectively by wrapping the victim with a blanket or coat. Often, fires can be extinguished by using a carbon dioxide fire extinguisher. Carbon dioxide does not burn. It is denser (heavier) than air and covers the flames, which smothers the fire.

3.3 Oxidation and Rusting

THINGS YOU WILL NEED:

- fine soapless steel wool (obtain from hard ware store)
- 10 medicine cups or small glasses
- tap water
- white vinegar
- household ammonia
- labels (stickies)
- forceps
- paper towels
- cooking oil
- teaspoon
- salt
- shiny steel (non-galvanized) nails
- notebook
- pen or pencil

Burning is an example of rapid oxidation. But not all oxidation is rapid, as you will see.

1. Obtain a roll or pad of fine soapless steel wool. Prepare three small balls of the steel wool.
2. Place three medicine cups or small glasses side by side. Put a ball of steel wool in each one. Fill the first one with tap water; the second with white vinegar, an acid; and the third with household ammonia, a base. Place labels (WATER, VINEGAR, AMMONIA) next to each container. Leave the steel wool in the liquids overnight.
3. Use forceps to remove the steel wool balls. Put them and their labels on several sheets of paper towels. Use the forceps to open and spread the steel wool.
4. Observe the steel wool for several days. Do you see any evidence of oxidation? Steel is mostly iron (Fe), which reacts

with oxygen to form iron oxides such as Fe_2O_3, a reddish-brown solid. (Sometimes, if the rust particles are very small, the rust will appear to be very dark. Spread a little out on a paper towel and allow it to dry. The rust color will become evident.)

Is there any evidence that iron has been oxidized? If so, which liquid(s) seem to promote oxidation? Which liquid(s), if any, seem to prevent oxidation?

5. Place six medicine cups or small glasses side by side. Fill five cups or glasses two-thirds of way with the following substances: tap water, white vinegar, household ammonia, cooking oil, and water mixed with a teaspoon of salt. Leave one cup empty, open to the air. Place labels (WATER, VINEGAR, AMMONIA, OIL, SALT, AIR) beside the appropriate cups.
6. Use steel wool to shine six steel (non-galvanized) nails. Place one nail in each cup. Fill another cup or glass with water. Put a galvanized nail in the water. Label this cup GALVANIZED NAIL. Galvanized nails are coated with zinc.

   Observe the nails daily for several days. Record any changes you see. Which substances seem to promote oxidation? Which substances seem to prevent or slow oxidation? What happened to the galvanized nail? Why do you think builders use galvanized nails when the nails will be exposed to the weather?
7. Repeat the experiment with the six cups or glasses that held tap water, white vinegar, household ammonia, cooking oil, salt water, and air. Instead of a nail, place a small amount of steel wool in each cup or vial.
8. Predict which cups or vials will show evidence that the steel is being oxidized, and which will show little or no evidence. After several days, compare results with your predictions. How well did you do?

3.4 A Look at Oxidation-Reduction Reactions

THINGS YOU WILL NEED:

- paper
- balance
- about 50 g of copper sulfate (get from science teacher or buy at a store that provides swimming pool chemicals)
- distilled water, rain-water, or soft water
- glass, plastic cup, or beaker
- stirring rod or coffee stirrer
- steel nail
- steel wool

To a chemist, oxidation involves more than reactions with oxygen. A chemist defines oxidation as a loss of electrons. A gain of electrons is called reduction. When something is oxidized (loses electrons), something else must be reduced (gains electrons).

1. Place a piece of paper on a balance pan. Weigh out 50 g of the blue crystals of copper sulfate ($CuSO_4 \bullet 5H_2O$) onto the paper. Copper sulfate consists of copper ions (Cu^{2+}), which have a charge of +2, combined with sulfate ions (SO_4^{2-}), which have a charge of -2.
2. Pour about 100 mL of distilled water, rainwater, or soft water into a glass, plastic cup, or beaker. Add the copper sulfate and stir until most of the blue crystals dissolve.
3. Steel is mostly iron (Fe). Find a steel nail that is taller than the container holding the copper sulfate solution. Rub the nail with some steel wool to make it bright and shiny. Then put the nail in the copper sulfate (Figure 13a).

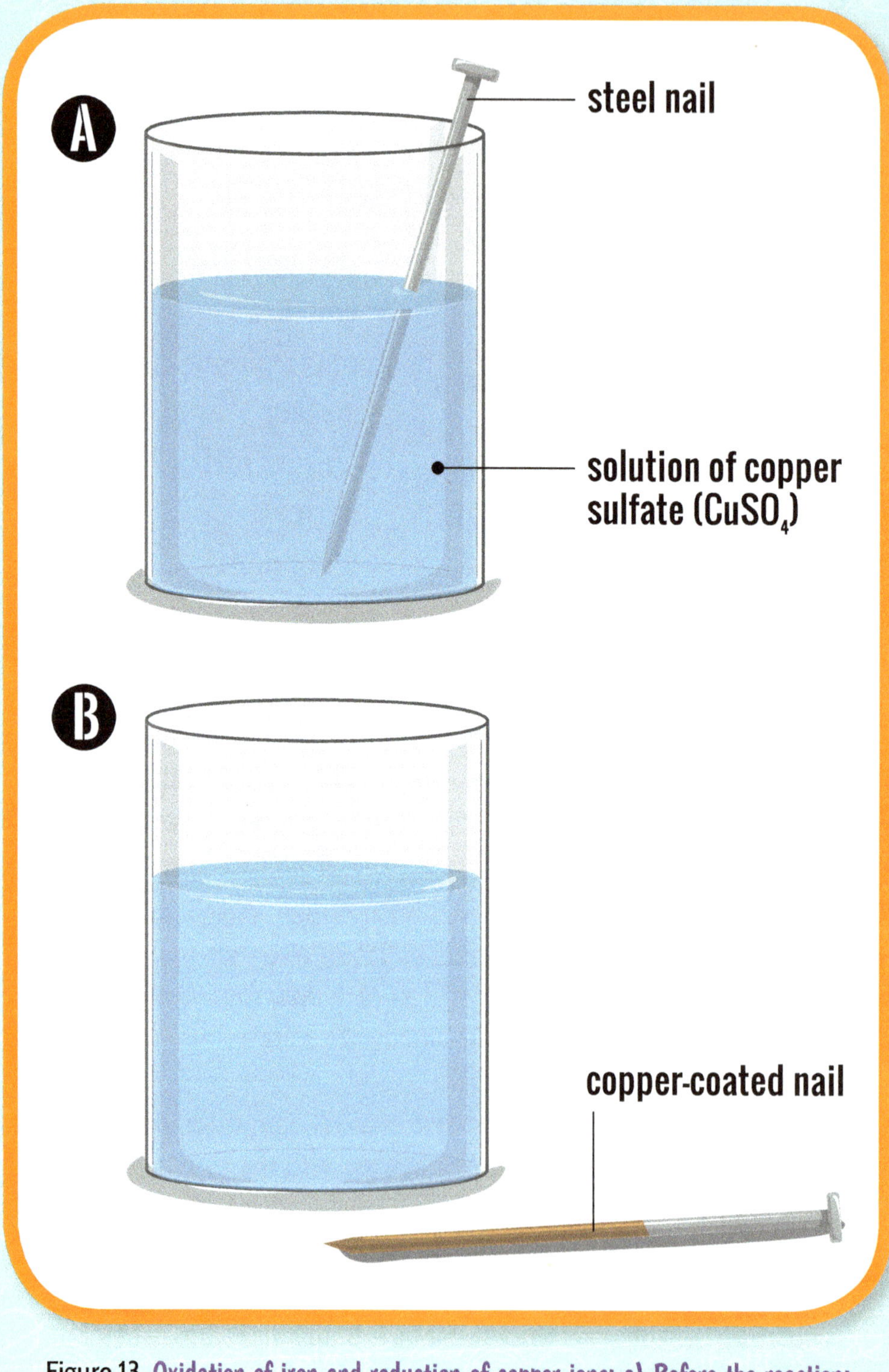

Figure 13. Oxidation of iron and reduction of copper ions: a) Before the reaction; b) After the reaction.

4. After an hour, remove the nail. Notice the reddish substance that has collected on the nail. It is copper (Figure 13b). Copper atoms (Cu) have no charge. The copper ions must have gained electrons to become copper atoms. The electrons came from the iron atoms, which were uncharged. The iron atoms became positively charged ions and dissolved in the solution. The equations below summarize what happened in this oxidation-reduction reaction.

$$Fe \rightarrow Fe^{2+} + 2e^-$$

$$Cu^{2+} + 2e^- \rightarrow Cu$$

$$Cu^{2+} + Fe \rightarrow Cu + Fe^{2+}$$

What was oxidized? What was reduced? (Sulfate ions are not shown because they are not involved in the reaction. Chemists call ions that are not involved in a reaction spectator ions.)

In Experiment 3.3, iron rusted under some conditions. The iron changed from uncharged atoms into positively charged ions. So the iron was oxidized. What do you think was reduced?

3.5 Oxygen in the Air

THINGS YOU WILL NEED:

- soapless pad of fine steel wool (obtain from hardware store)
- jar
- white vinegar
- water
- shallow plastic container
- ruler
- food coloring
- plastic gloves
- 4 tall jars with straight sides (some olive jars are good) or tall, wide test tubes
- pencil
- paper
- support for tubes (optional)
- marking pen or rubber bands
- ruler
- notebook

You have read that air is 21 percent oxygen. How do we know that to be true?

As you have seen, steel wool dipped in vinegar reacts with air to form iron oxide (rust). We can make use of that reaction to find out what fraction of air is oxygen.

1. Soak a soapless pad of fine steel wool overnight in a jar containing white vinegar and an equal volume of water.
2. Add water to a shallow plastic container to a depth of about 2 cm (1 in). Add a drop or two of food coloring to make the water more visible.
3. Put on plastic gloves. Pull a few strands of steel wool from the pad that has soaked in the vinegar solution. Roll them

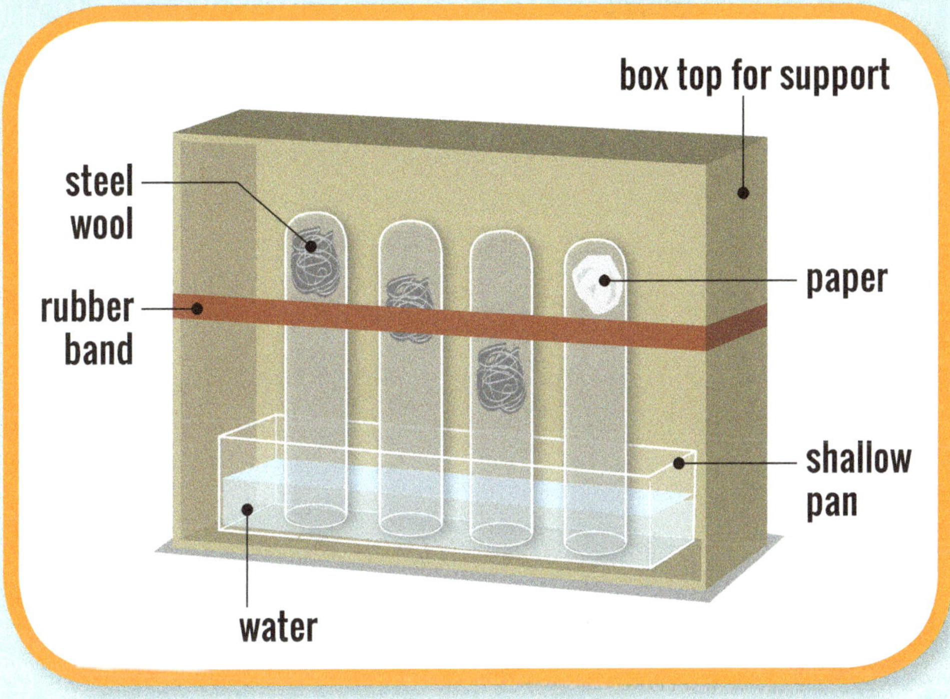

Figure 14. **An experiment can find out what fraction of air is oxygen.**

into a small loosely packed ball. Make three such balls from the steel wool. They should be slightly larger in diameter than the three tall narrow jars, such as olive jars, or tall, wide test tubes that will be used in the experiment.

4. Put a steel wool ball into each of three tall jars with straight sides or three large test tubes. Using a pencil, push one ball all the way to the bottom of one jar or tube. Push a second ball about three-fourths of the way to the bottom of a second jar or tube. Push a third ball about halfway down another jar or tube. Make another ball from a small sheet of paper and push it to the bottom of a fourth jar or tube.
5. Turn the four jars or tubes upside down. Place them side by side in the shallow pan of colored water as shown in Figure 14. If the

tubes are "tippy," fasten them to a support such as a shallow box so that they remain upright.

6. Leave the jars or tubes for twenty-four hours. Then mark the water level in each tube with a marking pen or rubber bands. Leave them for several more hours. Does the water continue to rise? If it does, wait until it stops rising. Then mark the new levels.
7. Look closely at the steel wool in the jars or tubes. Has it rusted? What has happened to the oxygen that was in the jar or tube? Why did the water not rise in one jar or tube? What was the purpose of that tube? Did the position of the steel wool affect the height to which the water rose?
8. Use a ruler to measure the water level in each tube. What is the ratio of the height of the water level to the total length of the jar or tube? Assume that all the oxygen in the jar or tube reacted with the steel wool. What fraction or percent of air is oxygen according to your experiment? For example, suppose the water rose 3 cm in a tube that is 15 cm long. The ratio height of water to height of tube is:

$$\frac{3.0 \text{ cm}}{15.0 \text{ cm}} = \frac{1.0}{5.0} = 0.20 = 20\%$$

If you did this experiment carefully, you probably found that the water level rose about the same fraction of the total height in each tube or jar. How did your measurement of the percentage of oxygen in air compare with the 21 percent mentioned earlier?

If your results are close to 21 percent, it indicates that steel wool rusting in a closed container combines with all the oxygen available. Suppose you replace the steel wool with a burning candle. Do you think the results will be the same?

FOR A SCIENCE FAIR PROJECT IDEA

- Show that the volume of the steel wool was negligible compared to the volume of the tube.

3.6 Measure the Percent of Oxygen in Air

THINGS YOU WILL NEED:

- **an adult**
- shallow plastic container
- food coloring
- water
- clay
- 4 birthday candles
- matches
- 4 tall jars or tubes as described in Experiment 3.5
- ruler
- notebook

You will be working with burning candles in this experiment. Therefore, you should work with an adult.

Do you think a burning candle can be used to measure the fraction of air that is oxygen? Let's find out.

1. Set up the shallow container and 2-cm-deep colored water as you did in the previous experiment.
2. Make four small clay disks to support four birthday candles. Place the upright candles and clay supports on the bottom of the container. **Ask an adult** to light the four candles. Place the four jars or tubes you used before over the burning candles. Try to vary the time you take to bring the open ends of the tubes over the candles. What happens to the candles?

   How long does it take the water levels to reach their maximum heights in this experiment?
3. Measure the height of the water in each tube. What is the ratio of the water level to the total length of the tube or jar

for each tube or jar? Is it the same in each case? Does the amount of water that entered a tube or jar seem to be related to the time it took you to lower the tube or jar over the candle?

Assume the burning candle uses up all the oxygen in each of the four cases. What fraction of air is oxygen according to your results for each tube or jar? Are your results consistent?

3.7 Air Expansion and Heating

THINGS YOU WILL NEED:

- **an adult**
- balloons
- 1-liter plastic bottle
- hot water faucet
- refrigerator
- birthday candle
- clay
- shallow plastic container
- soap
- water
- ruler
- matches
- tall jar or test tube
- frozen juice can
- short birthday candle
- shears
- strong rubber band

You probably found that your results in Experiment 3.6 were not very consistent. You might have found that oxygen makes up as much as 30 percent of air or as little as 10 percent. One explanation for the inconsistency might be the fact that air expands when heated.

1. Pull the mouth of a balloon over the top of an empty one-liter plastic bottle. Then hold the bottle under hot water pouring from a faucet (Figure 15a). What happens to the balloon?
2. Place the bottle and attached balloon in a refrigerator for ten minutes. What happens to the balloon?
3. Place a birthday candle with a clay holder on the bottom of a shallow plastic container. Add soapy water to a depth of about 2 cm. Brush away any bubbles near the candle.
4. **Ask an adult** to light the candle. Once the candle is burning brightly, quickly lower a tall jar or test tube down over the

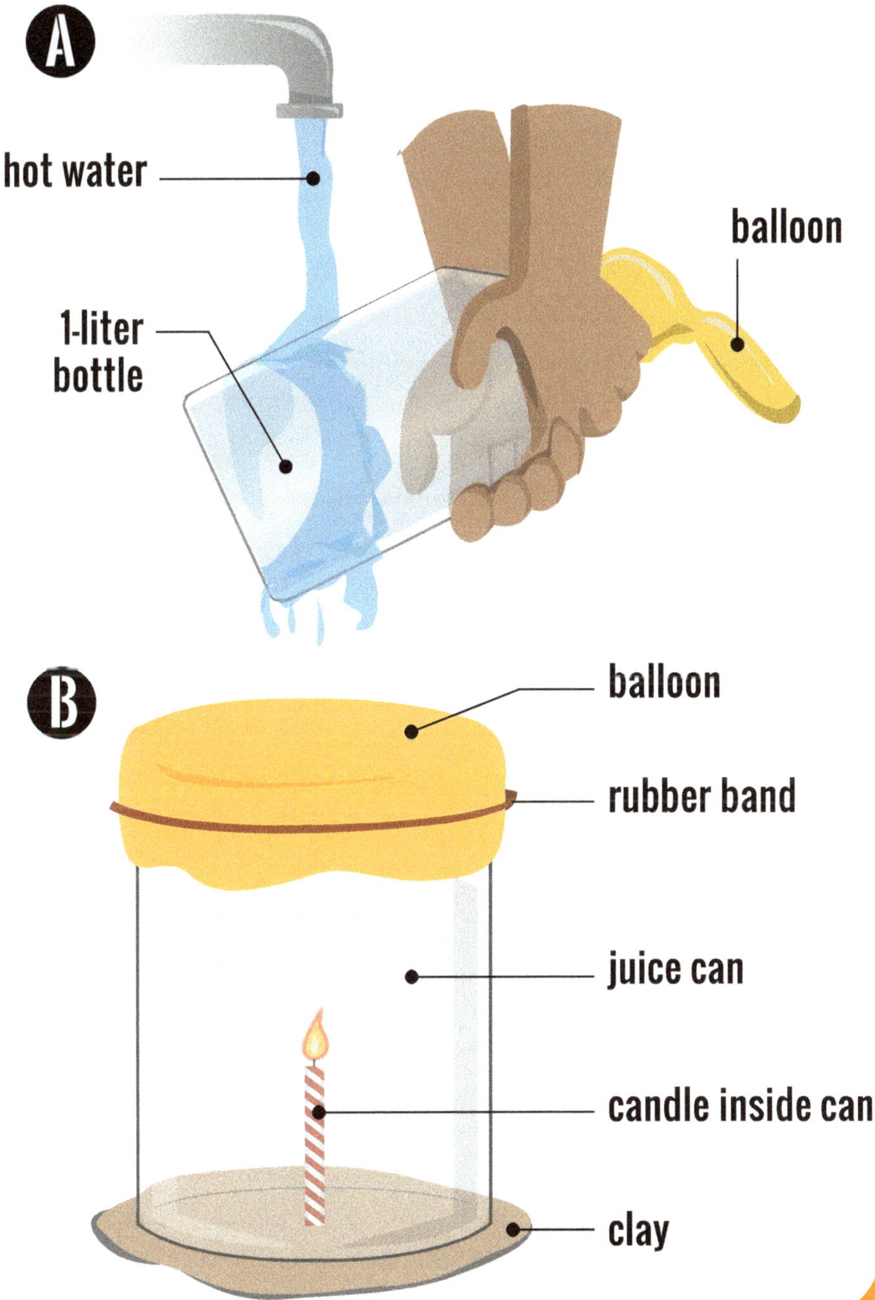

Figure 15. Two experiments show that air expands when heated and shrinks when cooled.

burning candle. Look for bubbles of gas emerging from the bottom of the jar or tube. Why would the air in the jar expand and form bubbles in the water? What will happen when the candle goes out and the gas in the jar cools?

It takes time to lower the tube over the candle. This can affect the amount of air left in the tube that hasn't expanded when the tube reaches the water. If the tube is lowered slowly, most of the air in the tube has expanded by the time it reaches the water. As a result, there will be few, if any, bubbles. The amount the air in the tube expands before it reaches the water affects the amount of water that enters the tube to replace the air that escapes. Consequently, the height to which the water rises can vary considerably.

To prove that the air in the tube does expand when heated, you can do another experiment.

5. Remove both top and bottom from an empty frozen juice can.
6. Stick a short birthday candle in the center of a thick disk of modeling clay. The diameter of the disk should be larger than the diameter of the juice can. The candle must be short so that its flame does not reach the top of the juice can, which will be covered with a rubber membrane.
7. Hold the neck of a large balloon between your thumb and index finger. Let the rest of the balloon hang from your thumb and finger. Use shears to cut off the bottom half of the balloon. Stretch the bottom half of the balloon across the top of the juice can. Use a strong rubber band to keep it stretched and in place (Figure 15b).
8. Have **an adult** light the candle. Wait until the candle is burning well. Then quickly bring the can down over the candle and press it into the clay so that no air can escape.

What happens to the rubber membrane? Does it bulge outward as the air expands? Does it contract as the air cools?

9. Repeat the experiment several times. Vary the speed at which you lower the can. Does the rubber membrane bulge out less when you lower the can slowly?

An Experiment About Oxygen in the Air

Jan Baptist van Helmont (1577–1644), a Flemish physician, carried out an experiment that is related to the amount of oxygen in air. He put a mouse and a burning candle under a large jar (Figure 16a). The candle went out, but the mouse continued to breathe and move (Figure 16b). The experiment provides some clear evidence about a burning candle in a closed space. A burning candle does not use all the oxygen that is available in the air. If it did, the mouse would not have survived.

Figure 16. a) Van Helmont put a mouse and a burning candle in a large sealed jar. b) The mouse continued to live after the flame went out.

3.8 A Hypothesis About Oxygen

THINGS YOU WILL NEED:

- soapless pad of steel wool (obtain from hardware store)
- white vinegar
- water
- shallow plastic container
- ruler
- food coloring
- plastic gloves
- 4 tall narrow jars (olive jars are good) or tall, wide test tubes
- pencil
- 4 birthday candles
- clay
- support for tubes (optional)
- marking pen or rubber bands
- notebook

The two previous experiments and van Helmont's experiment suggest that a burning candle in a closed space does not use all the oxygen. These results lead to a hypothesis. If steel wool in a jar or test tube is placed over a burning candle, the water should continue to rise for several hours after the flame goes out. If the burning candle does not use all the oxygen available, the steel wool should combine with the oxygen that is left. Water should move up the tube to replace the oxygen that combines with the steel wool. You can do an experiment to test this hypothesis.

1. Repeat Experiment 3.6 **under adult supervision**, but this time push a ball of steel wool that has been soaked in vinegar to the bottom of all four tubes or jars.
2. Put each jar or tube over a burning candle that has been supported with a small lump of clay. After the candle goes

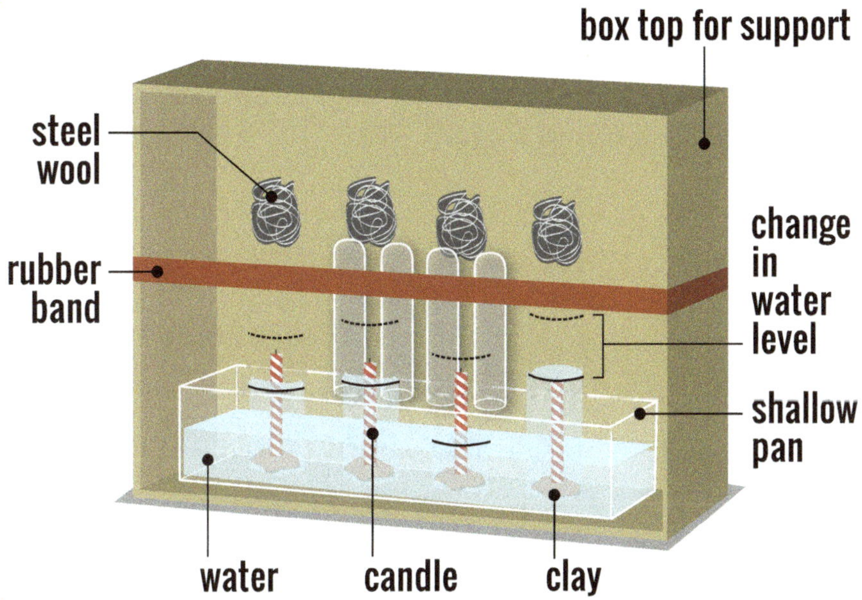

Figure 17. **Testing a hypothesis. The solid lines on the tubes show the water levels shortly after the candles went out. The dotted lines show the water levels twenty-four hours later.**

out and the water stops rising, mark the water level in each tube with a marking pen or a rubber band.

3. After twenty-four hours, look at the water levels again. Look closely at the steel wool. Does the steel wool's appearance show that it has reacted with oxygen? Did the water continue to rise?
4. When the water stops rising, mark the new water level in each tube or jar. Use a ruler to measure the change in the water levels (Figure 17). How do the changes in the water levels in the four tubes compare? Are they the same? How do the changes in water level in this experiment compare with those you found in Experiment 3.5?

Do the results of this experiment confirm the hypothesis? Did the candle use up all the oxygen when it burned?

On the basis of your results, what fraction of the oxygen in the air remains after the candle goes out? What fraction of the oxygen was used by the burning candle before it went out?

IDEAS FOR A SCIENCE FAIR PROJECT

- **Use the last few experiments to demonstrate that a burning candle cannot be used to measure the percentage of oxygen in air.**
- **Use the reaction of steel wool with oxygen to show that the percentage of oxygen in air can be measured quite accurately.**

Chapter 4

Identifying Substances

Chemists help us know more about the substances around us. Does the drinking water contain any toxins, such as lead? Is the farmland rich in nitrogen? Substances are identified by testing them in various ways. Physical tests, such as finding melting points, boiling points, density, and solubility, are sometimes used. But chemical tests are also used. You will examine some of those chemical tests in this chapter.

Before substances can be tested, they often have to be separated from the mixture in which they are found. A mixture contains two or more different substances. Sometimes the mixture is heterogeneous. This means that you can see the different substances in the mixture. For example, a mixture of salt and pepper is a heterogeneous mixture. You can easily see the black particles of pepper and the white particles of salt. But some mixtures are homogeneous. Even though the mixture contains more than one substance, it looks the same throughout.

If you add a teaspoonful of salt to a cup of water, you have, at first, a heterogeneous mixture. You can see the salt resting at the bottom of the water. But if you stir the mixture, the salt disappears. The mixture becomes homogeneous. Simply by looking, you cannot tell the difference between water and salt water.

Substances such as salt or sugar disappear in water, forming a homogeneous liquid. We call the mixture a solution. The substances in a solution can be separated. In the next experiment you will see how this is done.

4.1 Identifying Substances in a Solution

THINGS YOU WILL NEED:

- kosher (pure) salt
- water
- cooking pan
- a cup, preferably a metal one
- aluminum foil
- ice cubes
- stove
- sink

1. Add a tablespoon of kosher salt to a cup of water. Stir the mixture until the salt disappears. You now have a solution of salt and water.

   A chemist would use an apparatus similar to that shown in Figure 18a to separate the salt from the water. When the solution in the flask is heated, it boils. The water vapor rises and enters the condenser, where it cools, changes back to a liquid, and collects in the flask at the lower end of the condenser. The salt remains in the distilling flask. The process is called distillation.

   You probably do not have the chemical apparatus shown. However, you can understand how the process works using materials available in your kitchen.
2. Pour the salt solution into a cooking pan. Wash your hands. Then dip a finger into the salt solution. Bring that finger to your tongue. You should be able to taste the salt.
3. Place an empty cup in the center of the pan.
4. Cover the cooking pan with a sheet of aluminum foil as shown in Figure 18b. Place a few ice cubes in the center of the aluminum foil.

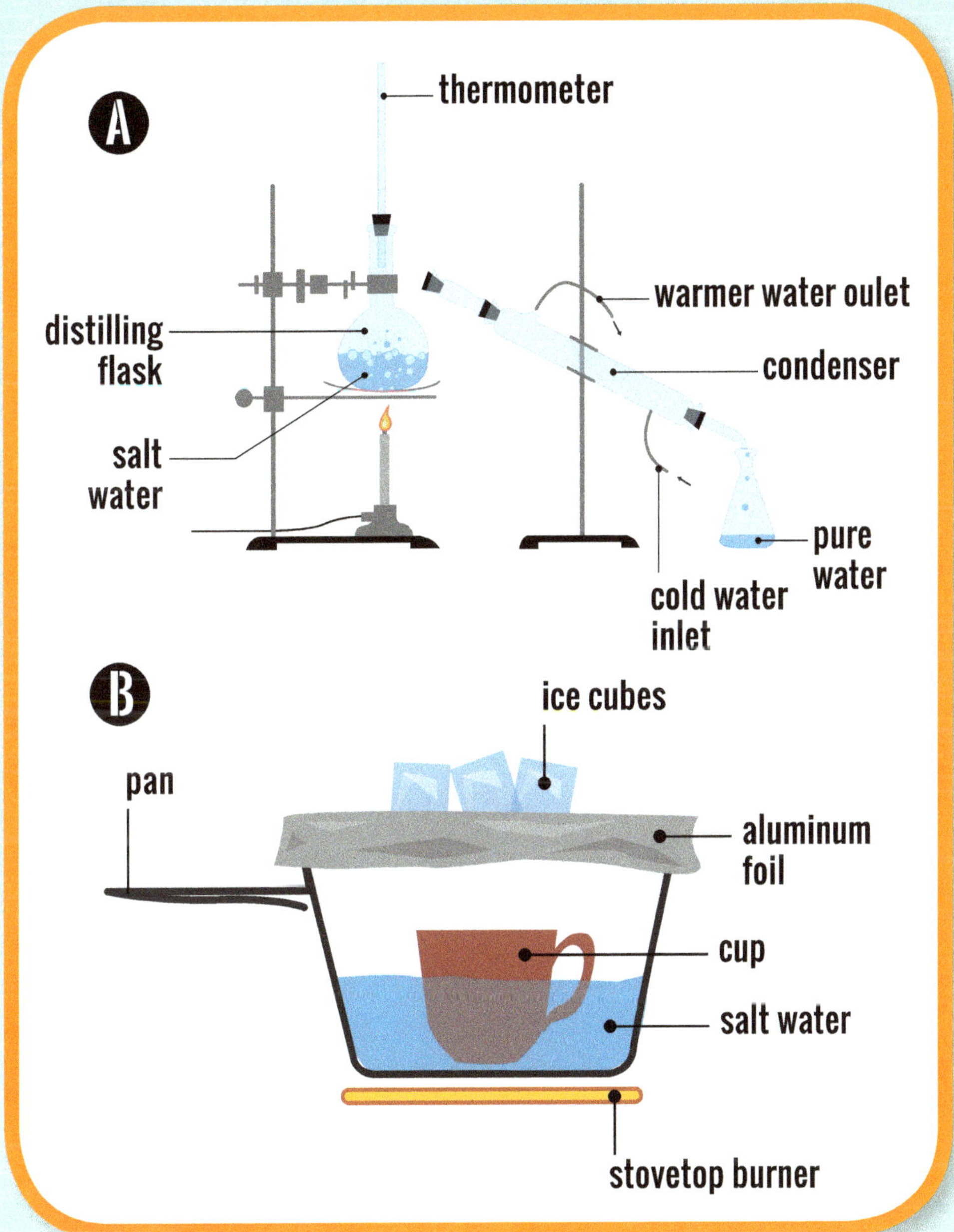

Figure 18. a) A chemist's distillation apparatus b) Your distillation apparatus

5. **Ask an adult** to place the pan on a stove and heat the salt water solution. Let the water boil until most of the ice has melted. If you have a metal cup in the pan, you may be able to hear water dripping into the cup.
6. Have **the adult** place the pan in a sink and carefully remove the aluminum foil, melted ice, and the cup.
7. Wash your hands. Then use a finger to taste the liquid that collected in the cup. Is it salty?

   What liquid do you think is in the cup? What do you think was the purpose of the ice on the aluminum foil cover?

FOR A SCIENCE FAIR PROJECT IDEA

- What is fractional distillation? How can it be used to separate two liquids such as isopropyl alcohol and water? **Under the supervision of a science teacher**, use fractional distillation to separate a one-to-one mixture of isopropyl alcohol and water. How can you identify the two liquids after separating them?

4.2 Identifying Solid Substances

THINGS YOU WILL NEED:

- steel thumbtacks
- paper
- magnet
- sawdust or wood shavings from a pencil sharpener
- glass or beaker
- water
- dining fork
- dry sand
- plastic cup or a glass beaker
- teaspoon
- kosher salt
- plastic cup
- plastic spoon or wooden coffee stirrer
- coffee filter
- large funnel
- tall vessel
- paper towels
- aluminum pie pan

1. Place a few steel thumbtacks on a sheet of paper. Bring a magnet near the thumbtacks. What happens? Are the thumbtacks magnetic (attracted to a magnet)?
2. Put some sawdust or wood shavings from a pencil sharpener in a glass or beaker. Add water. Do the wood particles sink or float in water? What does this tell you about the density of wood? Use a dining fork to skim off the wood particles. If you use wood shavings from a pencil sharpener, there will be some tiny black particles of pencil lead (graphite) in the water. Don't be concerned about them.
3. Put some sand in a plastic cup or a glass beaker. Add water. Is the sand soluble in water?

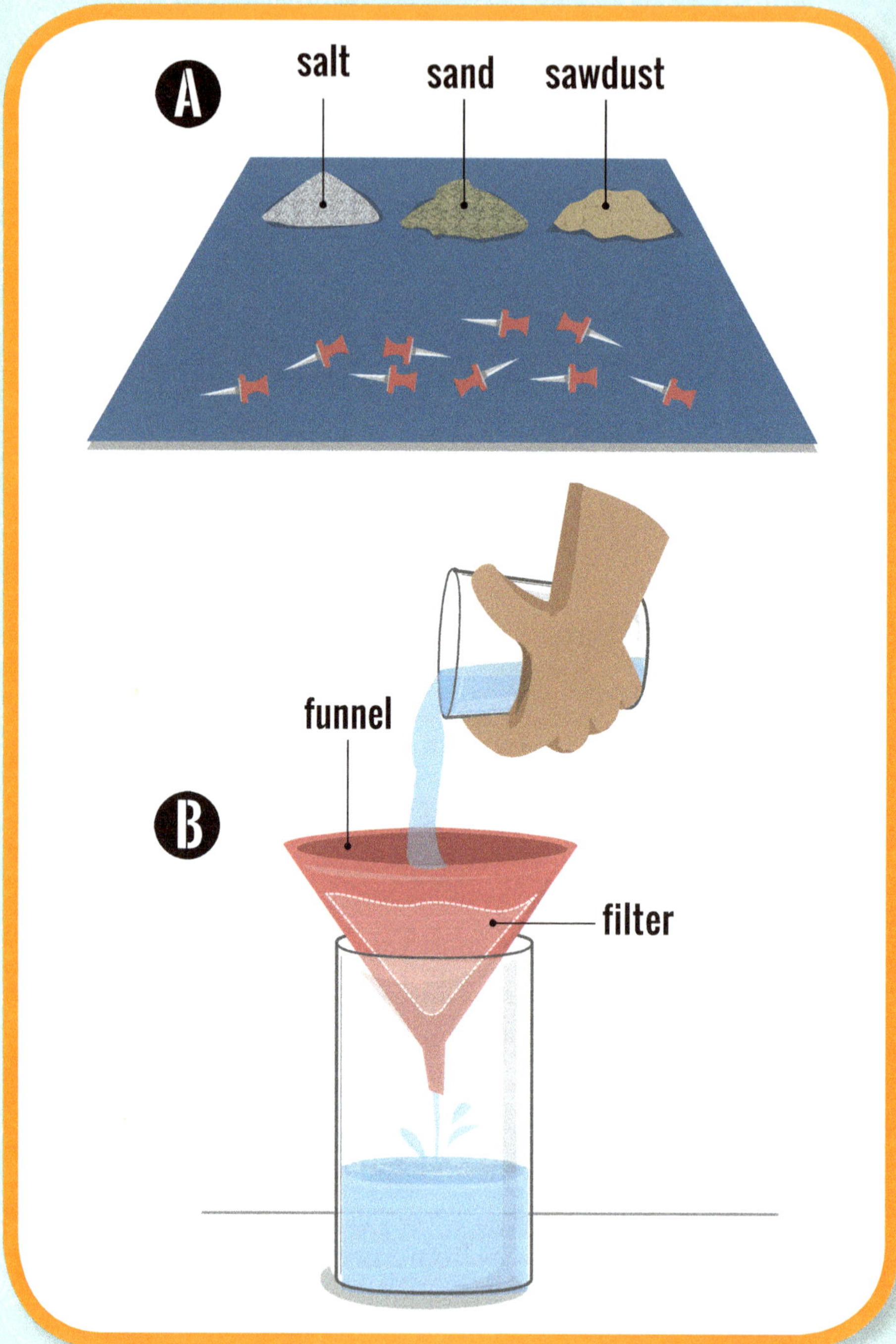

Figure 19. a) Substances to be mixed b) Place a filter in a funnel. Pour the wet mixture onto the filter. Collect the liquid (filtrate) in a glass or cup.

4. On a sheet of paper place a teaspoonful each of salt, sand, and sawdust or wood shavings. Add a few thumbtacks and stir to make a mixture (Figure 19a).
5. Use a magnet to separate one component from the mixture.
6. Pour the remaining parts of the mixture into a plastic cup. Fill the cup about halfway with water. Stir with a plastic spoon or wooden coffee stirrer. You have added another component (water) to the mixture. But the water will help you separate parts of the mixture. Which component has dissolved in the water? Which component can be skimmed off the surface of the water?
7. After skimming off part of the mixture, place a coffee filter in a large funnel. Put the funnel in a tall vessel. Pour the mixture into the coffee filter (Figure 19b). Let the liquid pass through the filter into the glass. Add more water to rinse any solid that remains in the cup or on the filter paper.
8. When all the liquid has passed through the filter, remove the filter from the funnel. Place the filter and its contents on several layers of paper towels. Let the solid and filter dry. After they have dried, identify the solid.
9. Pour the liquid that passed through the filter onto an aluminum pie pan. Set the pan in a warm place and allow the water to evaporate. What remains on the pie plate after the water evaporates?

4.3 Identifying Starch

THINGS YOU WILL NEED:

- **an adult**
- plastic gloves
- safety goggles
- 2 eyedroppers
- tincture of iodine
- water
- corn starch
- saucers
- raw potato
- cooked potato
- white bread
- milk
- white meat, such as chicken breast
- sheet of writing paper
- teaspoon
- sugar
- unsalted cracker
- notebook
- pen or pencil
- detergent
- hot water

Wear plastic gloves and safety goggles while doing this experiment. Make sure you have an adult present to supervise.

It is easy to identify the presence of starch. It turns a very dark blue when in contact with iodine.

1. Prepare a dilute iodine solution by mixing about 10 drops of tincture of iodine with 30 drops of water. **Be careful handling iodine. It is a poison, and it stains flesh. Do not put anything with iodine on it into or near your mouth or eyes!**
2. Place half a teaspoon of corn starch on a saucer. Add a drop of the iodine solution. What do you observe?
3. In separate saucers, place a slice of raw potato, some cooked potato, a piece of white bread, some milk, some chopped white meat such as chicken breast, a piece from a sheet of writing paper, half a teaspoon of sugar, and an unsalted cracker.

4. Test each sample by adding a drop of the iodine solution. Record your results in your notebook. Which of the substances you tested contained starch?
5. Discard the samples you tested and wash the saucers using detergent and hot water.

4.4 Identifying Iodized Salt

THINGS YOU WILL NEED:

- graduated cylinder or metric measuring cup
- 3% hydrogen peroxide
- glass or a clear plastic cup
- measuring spoons
- iodized salt
- clock or watch
- corn starch

Table salt, which is sodium chloride (NaCl), often contains small amounts of sodium iodide (NaI). The table salt will be labeled "Iodized salt." Your thyroid gland, located in your neck, needs iodide ions (I^-) to function properly. That is why sodium iodide is often added to ordinary salt.

In the previous experiment, you saw starch turn a very dark blue color when iodine was added. You can use that fact in reverse to identify the iodide ion present in iodized salt. But first, you must change the iodide ion to iodine. This can be done by adding hydrogen peroxide to the iodized salt. The hydrogen peroxide will oxidize the iodide to iodine (the iodide ions [I^-] lose electrons to become iodine atoms). The atoms then pair up to form iodine molecules (I_2). The electrons are gained by the oxygen in the hydrogen peroxide, which changes to water. See the chemical equation below.

$$2I^- + H_2O_2 + 2H^+ \rightarrow I_2 + 2H_2O$$

1. Pour 60 mL (2 oz) of 3% hydrogen peroxide into a glass or a clear plastic cup.
2. Add 2 tablespoons of iodized salt and stir to dissolve as much of the salt as possible.
3. Wait about three minutes. Then add 1/4 teaspoon of corn starch and stir. What evidence is there that iodine is present?

4. Repeat the experiment using kosher salt. Kosher salt is pure salt to which nothing has been added. Do you expect the starch to turn color after hydrogen peroxide is added to the kosher salt solution? What do you find?

Try This for Fun

You might tell someone that you can change the color of a liquid from cloudy to blue by simply adding a small amount of corn starch. What will you have to do ahead of time?

4.5 Identifying a Simple Sugar

THINGS YOU WILL NEED:

- **an adult**
- graduated cylinder or metric measuring cup
- honey or corn syrup
- Diastix (purchase at a drugstore)
- saucers
- water
- sucrose (table sugar)
- milk
- variety of juices, such as grape, orange, apple
- raw and cooked potatoes
- unsalted cracker
- bread
- cooked white chicken meat
- teaspoon
- iodine solution (see Experiment 4.3)
- eyedropper
- medicine cup
- plastic gloves
- safety goggles
- corn starch
- toothpick

Wear plastic gloves and safety goggles while doing this experiment. Make sure you have an adult present to supervise.

Ordinary table sugar is called sucrose. Its molecules are large. From its chemical formula ($C_{12}H_{22}O_{11}$), you can see that each sucrose molecule contains 45 atoms. Sucrose molecules in your food are broken apart by enzymes in your stomach and intestine. They are changed into simpler sugars (glucose and fructose). Both these sugars have the same chemical formula ($C_6H_{12}O_6$). However, they have different properties because the atoms in the molecules are arranged differently. Compounds that have the same formula but different properties are called isomers.

In your intestine, glucose is absorbed into your blood, which carries it to the cells of your body. There it is oxidized to provide the energy you need to live. People who suffer from diabetes (diabetics) are unable to use glucose properly. As a result, their urine often contains glucose.

Diastix can be purchased at a drugstore. These plastic sticks are used by diabetics to test for glucose in their urine. Diastix are the easiest way to test for glucose. Just dip the stick in a sample of liquid that you think may contain glucose. The sticks have a chemical on one end that changes color in the presence of glucose. The color indicates the concentration of the sugar in the liquid.

1. Pour about 5 mL of honey or corn syrup into a saucer. Add about 10 mL of water. Dip the chemical end of a Diastix into the liquid. Follow the directions on the bottle to test for glucose. Does the honey or syrup contain glucose? From the test strip, can you determine the concentration of glucose in the sweet liquid?
2. Repeat the experiment using 10 mL of a saturated solution of sucrose (table sugar). Does this sugar solution contain any glucose?
3. In separate saucers, place a few milliliters of milk and a variety of juices, such as grape juice, orange juice, apple juice, and so on. Test with Diastix. Do any of these liquids contain glucose?
4. Crush or pour samples of raw and cooked potatoes, an unsalted cracker, bread, and cooked white chicken meat onto separate saucers. Add a teaspoonful of warm water to each sample and stir. Then use Diastix to test for glucose. What do you conclude?
5. Chew an unsalted cracker for two or three minutes. Give it time to react with the saliva in your mouth. As you chew, does the cracker begin to have a sweet taste? Saliva contains amylase, an enzyme that breaks starch into sucrose. Sucrose is what you may taste. Can it break the sucrose into glucose?
6. To find out, spit out two samples of the unsalted cracker that you have thoroughly chewed onto separate saucers. Mix each of these samples with a little water. **Put on plastic gloves and safety goggles.**

Remember iodine is poisonous! Then use an eyedropper to test one sample with a drop of iodine solution. Test the second sample with a Diastix. Did the thoroughly chewed cracker still contain starch? Did it contain any glucose?

7. In a medicine cup, mix 1/2 teaspoon of corn starch with an equal amount of honey or corn syrup. Add a teaspoon of water and stir the mixture with a toothpick. Pour a small amount of the mixture onto a saucer and test with a Diastix.
8. Add a drop of iodine solution to the mixture. Can you get a positive test for glucose when the sugar is mixed with starch? Can you get a positive test for starch when the starch is mixed with glucose?

Ideas for a Science Fair Project

- **Can Diastix be used to test for other simple sugars such as fructose, galactose, and mannose? Design and carry out experiments to find out.**
- **Sometimes medicinal pills use starch to bind solids together. Do you think aspirin tablets contain starch? Design and conduct an experiment to find out.**
- **Do some research to find out how chemists test for larger sugar molecules such as sucrose, lactose, and maltose.**

4.6 Identifying Hydrogen Peroxide

THINGS YOU WILL NEED:

- pad of soapless, fine steel wool (obtain from hardware store)
- jar
- vinegar
- graduated cylinder or metric measuring cup
- clear plastic or glass cup
- 3% hydrogen peroxide

You used hydrogen peroxide (H_2O_2) to test for the iodide ion found in iodized salt. There is also a test to identify hydrogen peroxide. To carry out the test you will first have to prepare some iron acetate solution. You can do that quite easily. The iron acetate you need is ferrous acetate [$Fe(C_2H_3O_2)_2$]. [There are two kinds of iron ions—ferrous ions (Fe^{2+}), which have a charge of +2, and ferric ions (Fe^{3+}), which carry a charge of +3.]

1. Soak a pad of fine, soap-less steel wool in a jar of vinegar (acetic acid) for twenty-four hours. The iron (Fe) in the steel wool reacts with acetic acid to form ferrous acetate [$Fe(C_2H_3O_2)_2$].
2. Now that you have some ferrous acetate, pour about 10 mL of it into a clear plastic or glass cup. Add an equal volume of hydrogen peroxide. What happens?

   The deep reddish brown color of the product—ferric hydroxide [$Fe(OH)_3$]—is a test for hydrogen peroxide. The hydrogen peroxide oxidizes the ferrous ions to ferric ions.

4.7 Identifying Vitamin C

THINGS YOU WILL NEED:

- **an adult**
- teaspoon
- corn starch
- steel cooking pan
- measuring cup
- water
- stove
- clear jar
- plastic gloves
- safety goggles
- eyedropper
- tincture of iodine
- 500 mg tablet of vitamin C
- cup or saucer
- tablespoon
- orange juice, lemon juice, cranberry juice, and a variety of fruit and vegetable juices

Vitamin C, ascorbic acid ($C_6H_8O_6$), is a substance essential to good health. Lack of the vitamin causes scurvy, a very serious disease. Scurvy was common among sailors up through the nineteenth century. To prevent the disease, they began to eat citrus fruits such as oranges and lemons, rich sources of vitamin C.

Wear plastic gloves and safety goggles while doing this experiment. Make sure you have an adult present to supervise.

1. Prepare a starch solution. Place 1/2 teaspoon of cornstarch in a steel cooking pan. Add 1 cup of water.
2. **Ask an adult** to heat and stir the mixture on a stove to dissolve as much of the starch as possible. Let the solution cool.
3. To prepare the test solution, put 1 teaspoon of the starch solution into a clear jar. Add 1 cup of water. Put on plastic gloves and goggles. Then use an eyedropper to add 4 drops

of tincture of iodine to the jar. **Remember iodine is a poison!** Do not get it near your mouth or eyes. The test solution, as you might expect, will turn blue.

4. **Ask the adult** to use a spoon to crush a 500 mg tablet of vitamin C in a saucer or cup. Add 1 cup of water and stir to make a solution of vitamin C (ascorbic acid).
5. Place 2 tablespoons of the test solution in a cup or saucer. Add 2 drops of the vitamin C solution and stir. What happens to the color of the test solution?
6. Test other substances for vitamin C. You might try drops of orange juice, lemon juice, cranberry juice, and a variety of fruit and vegetable juices that you think might contain vitamin C. Which substances contain vitamin C? Which do not?

Science Supply Companies

Arbor Scientific
PO Box 2750
Ann Arbor, MI 48106-2750
(800) 367-6695
arborsci.com

Carolina Biological Supply Co.
PO Box 6010
Burlington, NC 27215-3398
(800) 334-5551
carolina.com

Connecticut Valley Biological Supply Co., Inc.
82 Valley Road
PO Box 326
Southampton, MA 01073
(800) 628-7748
ctvalleybio.com

Educational Innovations, Inc.
5 Francis J. Clarke Circle
Bethel, CT 06801
(203) 748-3224
teachersource.com

Fisher Science Education
300 Industry Drive
Pittsburgh, PA 15275
(800) 955-1177
fishersci.com

Frey Scientific
80 Northwest Boulevard
Nashua, NH 03061-3000
(800) 225-3739
freyscientific.com

Nasco
901 Janesville Avenue
Fort Atkinson, WI 53538
(800) 558-9595
enasco.com/science

Scientifics Direct
532 Main Street
Tonawanda, NY 14150
(800) 818-4955
scientificsonline.com

Ward's Science
5100 West Henrietta Road
PO Box 92912
Rochester, NY 14692-9012
(800) 962-2660
wardsci.com

Glossary

acid A substance that tastes sour, contains hydrogen, turns blue litmus paper red, and neutralizes bases.

atom The smallest particle of an element.

base (alkali) A substance that has a bitter taste, feels slippery, turns red litmus paper blue, and neutralizes acids.

Brownian motion The jiggling motion of small particles, such as smoke particles or pollen grains, when they are struck by moving molecules of air or water.

chemical change The formation of at least one new substance during a chemical reaction. Atoms are rearranged, new molecules are formed, and energy is usually absorbed or released.

compound A substance made up of two or more elements.

covalent compound A compound in which the atoms share electrons.

diffusion The slow movement of one substance into another.

distillation A process in which a solution is heated and the vapors condense to separate the substances in the solution.

electron A particle found in atoms that has a negative charge. It is much smaller than a proton.

elements Substances that cannot be broken down into simpler substances. They contain only one kind of atom.

endothermic reaction A chemical reaction in which heat is absorbed and temperature decreases.

exothermic reaction A chemical reaction in which heat is produced and temperature increases.

heterogeneous mixture A mixture in which different substances can be seen.

homogeneous mixture A mixture that looks the same throughout.

ion An atom that has a positive or negative charge because it has lost or gained one or more electrons.

isomers Compounds that have the same chemical formula but different properties.

isotopes Atoms of the same element that differ in the number of neutrons in their nuclei.

law of conservation of matter Matter is never created or destroyed.

law of definite proportions Elements combine to form compounds in a fixed ratio by weight.

law of multiple proportions If two elements can form more than one compound, the weight ratio of the elements in one of those compounds will be a simple multiple of the weight ratio in the other compound or compounds.

mixture A combination of two or more different substances.

neutron A non-charged particle found in atomic nuclei. It weighs about the same as a proton.

nucleus (plural *nuclei*) The part at the center of an atom that contains most of the atom's weight. It is made up of protons and neutrons.

oxidation The chemical combination of oxygen with other elements to form compounds, or, more generally, the loss of electrons. When something is oxidized (loses electrons) something else must be reduced (gains electrons).

pH A measure of the concentration of hydrogen ions (H^+) in a substance.

proton A tiny, positively charged particle found in the nuclei of atoms.

reduction A gain of electrons. It is the opposite of oxidation.

scientific laws (laws of nature) Rules about nature that have no known exceptions.

solution A homogeneous mixture of one or more substances dissolved into another.

spectator ions Ions present but not involved in a chemical reaction.

Further Reading

Books

Ardley, Neil. *101 Great Science Experiments.* New York, NY: DK Ltd., 2014.

Buczynski, Sandy. *Designing a Winning Science Fair Project.* Ann Arbor, MI: Cherry Lake Publishing, 2014.

Cobb, Vicki. *Science Experiments You Can Eat.* New York, NY: Harper, 2016.

Henneberg, Susan. *Creating Science Fair Projects with Cool New Digital Tools.* New York, NY: Rosen Central, 2014.

Mercer, Bobby. *Junk Drawer Chemistry: 50 Awesome Experiments that Don't Cost a Thing.* Chicago, IL: Chicago Review Press, 2015.

O'Quinn, Amy M. *Marie Curie for Kids: Her Life and Scientific Discoveries, with 21 Activities and Experiments.* Chicago, IL: Chicago Review Press, 2017.

Thomas, Isabel. *Experiments with Materials.* Chicago, IL: Heinemann Raintree, 2016.

Websites

About.com: Education

chemistry.about.com/od/chemistryforkids

Lots of chemistry activities for kids.

Brain Pop

brainpop.com/science/scientificinquiry/scientificmethod

Have fun learning about the scientific method.

Exploratorium: Science Snacks

exploratorium.edu/snacks/subject/chemistry

A great set of links to more chemistry activities and facts.

Index